FIRST-COURSE DISHES

—————— • ——————

Great care should be taken, that,
between the first and second courses, no
more time is allowed to elapse than is
necessary, for fear that the company in
the dining-roiom lose all relish for what
has yet to come of the dinner.

Isabella Beeton 1861

Left: *Cucumber Cassolettes (page 36)* and
Melon with Parma Ham (page 16)
Below: *Stuffed Eggs (page 27)*

FRUIT DISHES

GRAPEFRUIT BASKETS

———— *4 helpings* ————

2 large firm grapefruit
1 × 5cm/2 inch segment ripe
   Charentais *or* Ogen melon
225g/8oz canned pineapple cubes

1 orange
4 maraschino cherries
white *or* brown sugar *or* 4 × 10ml
   spoons/4 dessertspoons
   medium-dry sherry

DECORATION

mint sprigs

Cut the grapefruit in half crossways, and remove the pips. Snip out the cores with scissors. Remove the flesh from the halved skins, and snip out the membranes in the skins. Keep the halved skins aside, and put the flesh in a basin. Cut the melon flesh into 2.5 cm/1 inch cubes, drain the pineapple, and prepare the orange like the grapefruit. Halve the cherries. Mix all the fruit with the grapefruit flesh in the basin. Sweeten slightly if desired, or add the sherry. Pile the fruit (with any juice or sherry) back into the grapefruit skins. Chill before serving. Serve decorated with mint sprigs.

GRAPEFRUIT COCKTAIL

———— *6 helpings* ————

3 grapefruit
50g/2oz sugar
3 × 15ml spoons/3 tablespoons
   boiling water

2 × 15ml spoons/2 tablespoons
   medium-dry sherry

DECORATION

6 maraschino cherries
6 mint sprigs

Cut the grapefruit in half crossways and remove the pips. Snip out the cores with scissors. Remove the flesh from the halved skin, and put in a basin. Dissolve the sugar in the water, add the sherry and pour the mixture over the fruit. Cover and chill until ready to serve. Spoon into suitable glasses, and decorate with the cherries and sprigs of mint before serving.

CHERRY.

SPICED GRAPEFRUIT

4 helpings

2 large grapefruit
25g/1oz softened butter
25–50g/1–2oz brown sugar

½–1 × 5ml spoon/½–1 teaspoon
ground mixed spice

DECORATION

4 glacé *or* maraschino cherries

Cut the grapefruit in half crossways, and remove the pips. Snip out the cores with scissors. Spread the butter over the grapefruit, and sprinkle with the sugar and spice. Put under a hot grill for 4 minutes, or in a fairly hot oven at 200°C/400°F/Gas 6, for 10 minutes.

Decorate with the cherries, and serve at once.

Grapefruit Baskets

Avocado Pears with Prawns or Avocado Royale

— 4 helpings —

2 × 15ml spoons/2 tablespoons olive oil
2 × 15ml spoons/2 tablespoons distilled vinegar
a pinch each of salt and pepper
a little mixed French mustard (not Dijon)
2 large avocado pears

a pinch of sugar (optional)
½ clove of garlic (optional)
100g/4oz peeled prawns, fresh, frozen or canned
crisp lettuce leaves

GARNISH

lemon wedges

Blend the oil, vinegar, and seasonings together. Halve and stone the pears, and brush all over with a little of the dressing. Add the sugar and crush and add the garlic to the remaining dressing, if used. Toss the prawns in this; then spoon into the pear halves. Place on crisp lettuce leaves. Garnish with lemon wedges.

Note Frozen prawns should be squeezed gently before using to get rid of any excess moisture.

THE LEMON.

Avocado Pears and Soured Cream

— 4 helpings —

2 avocado pears
1 × 5ml spoon/1 teaspoon lemon juice
1 × 5ml spoon/1 teaspoon salt
2 × 5ml spoons/2 teaspoons caster sugar

1 × 2.5 ml spoon/½ teaspoon dry mustard
a pinch of paprika
150ml/¼ pint soured cream or smetana

Halve the pears lengthways and remove the stones. Scoop all the flesh out of the skins, and mash it with the lemon juice and half the salt. Replace the flesh in the shells. To make the dressing, mix all the remaining ingredients together until smooth. Top the pears with the dressing.

Avocado Pears Vinaigrette

— 4 helpings —

2 large, firm, ripe avocado pears
2 × 15ml spoons/2 tablespoons lemon juice

vinaigrette sauce

Make sure the pear are firm but ripe, and are not discoloured. If they show any signs of over-ripeness such as being soft or blackened, use them for a cooked dish.

Halve the pears lengthways and remove the stones. Brush the halved pears with lemon juice immediately to prevent discoloration. Serve 1 half pear per person, cut side uppermost on a small plate, with a special avocado spoon, stainless steel or silver teaspoon or a grapefruit spoon. Serve the vinaigrette sauce separately.

MELON

Melon makes a refreshing starter throughout the year. The varieties most often used are the Cantaloup, honeydew, Ogen, Charentais, and watermelon. Melon should always be served lightly chilled, but it should not be too cold or it loses its delicate flavour.

To serve a large Cantaloup or honeydew melon, cut it in half lengthways, then cut into segments and remove the seeds with a spoon. Serve 1 segment per person; a large melon should supply 8 segments.

Serve the melon with the flesh attached to the skin, or cut the flesh from the skin with a sharp knife but leave the skin underneath the melon segment. The melon flesh can then also be cut into small pieces which are easier to eat.

Smaller melons, such as Ogen and Charentais, should just be cut in half crossways, and the pips scooped out with a spoon. They serve 2 people as a rule, although they can be cut into quarters, to serve four.

Watermelon should be cut into suitably sized segments. Small spoons should be provided for removing the seeds, as well as knives and forks for cutting up the melon.

Ripe melons may not require any sugar, but sugar can be served separately, with chopped stem ginger or ground ginger, or with lemon or lime.

Avocado Pears with Prawns

MARINATED MELON

4 helpings

2 Ogen *or* Charentais melons   4 × 15ml spoons/4 tablespoons
                                     maraschino liqueur *or* port

Cut the melons in half crossways and scoop out the seeds. Spoon 1 × 15ml spoon/1 tablespoon of maraschino liqueur or port into the centre and chill for 1 hour before serving. Sugar can be served with the melons as well, if desired.

MELON WITH PARMA HAM

This is an elaborate dish using paper-thin slices of Parma or other smoked ham. For each person, serve 3 loosely rolled slices of ham arranged in a line alternately with 7 × 2.5cm/1 inch sticks of firm, ripe, green-fleshed melon.

PEAR, NUT, AND DATE SALAD

6 helpings

3 ripe dessert pears *or* 6 canned pear halves
1 × 15ml spoon/1 tablespoon lemon juice
1 small crisp lettuce
100g/4oz stoned dates

50g/2oz shelled walnuts
1 × 10ml spoon/1 dessertspoon chopped parsley
3 × 15ml spoons/3 tablespoons French dressing

If using fresh pears, peel and halve them, and remove the cores with a small spoon. Sprinkle lightly with the lemon juice to preserve the colour. If using canned pears, drain off the juice, and dry thoroughly. Wash the lettuce and dry thoroughly. Reserve 6 outside leaves and shred the rest. Mix with the dates, walnuts, and parsley. Add the dressing and toss lightly. Arrange a lettuce leaf on each of 6 individual plates and place the pear in the centre, with the cut side uppermost. Pile in the date mixture and chill lightly for 1 hour before serving.

THE WALNUT.

PEARS WITH STILTON

4 helpings

2 hard cooking pears	salt
50–75g/2–3oz Stilton cheese	fat for greasing
juice of 1 lemon	pepper

Peel the pears, cut in half lengthways, and remove the core and any pips. Cut each half pear into 3 or 4 thin slices lengthways. Cut the cheese into thin slices. Trim the cheese slices to fit the pears. Put to one side together with the trimmings. Simmer the pear slices in water with the lemon juice and a little salt. Remove them when softened at the edges but still firm in the centre.

· Grease a flat flameproof dish. Lay the pear slices in a circle with the narrower ends to the centre. Lay the cheese slices on top, and sprinkle with any cheese trimmings. Season very lightly with pepper (no salt). Grill under moderate heat for 3-5 minutes or until the cheese begins to bubble and brown. Serve at once.

Marinated Melon

VEGETABLE DISHES

RUSSIAN SALAD

4 helpings

1 small cooked cauliflower
3 boiled potatoes
2 tomatoes
50g/2oz ham *or* tongue (optional)
3 gherkins
a few lettuce leaves
4 × 15ml spoons/4 tablespoons
  peas

2 × 15ml spoons/2 tablespoons
  diced cooked carrot
2 × 15ml spoons/2 tablespoons
  diced cooked turnip
50g/2oz peeled prawns *or* shrimps
  (optional)
salt and pepper
3 × 15ml spoons/3 tablespoons
  mayonnaise

GARNISH

1 small diced cooked beetroot
50g/2oz smoked salmon, cut into
  strips (optional)
4 olives

1 × 15ml spoon/1 tablespoon
  capers
4 anchovy fillets (optional)

Break the cauliflower into small sprigs. Peel and dice the potatoes. Skin, de-seed, and dice the tomatoes. Cut the ham or tongue into small strips, if used. Chop the gherkins and shred the lettuce leaves. Put the vegetables, meat, and fish, if used, in layers in a salad bowl, sprinkling each layer with salt, pepper, and mayonnaise. Garnish with the remaining ingredients.

Opposite, from the top clockwise:
Stuffed Tomato Salad (page 24),
Pear, Nut and Date Salad (page 17) and
Russian Salad (page 19)

HOT STUFFED ARTICHOKE BASES

4 helpings

8 small cooked *or* canned artichoke
  bases

butter for greasing
round slices of fried bread *or* toast

STUFFING

200g/7oz cooked short-grain rice
4 × 15ml spoons/4 tablespoons
  grated Parmesan cheese
2 × 15ml spoons/2 tablespoons
  pine nut kernels

lemon juice
salt and pepper

Re-heat the artichoke bases by steaming for 6–8 minutes, or bake in a shallow dish in a cool oven under buttered paper for 15–18 minutes.

Meanwhile, make the stuffing. Mix together the rice, cheese, and pine nut kernels, a little lemon juice, and seasoning to taste, then heat gently.

Pile 1–2 × 15ml spoons/1–2 tablespoons of the hot stuffing in each artichoke base, and serve immediately on the fried bread or toast.

ARTICHOKES.

VEGETABLES À LA GRECQUE

4 helpings

500g/1lb vegetables (see **Note**)
½ × 2.5ml spoon/¼ teaspoon
  coriander seeds
1 clove of garlic
400g/13oz tomatoes
4 × 15ml spoons/4 tablespoons
  olive oil

2 × 15ml spoons/2 tablespoons
  lemon juice
150ml/6 fl oz water
1 bay leaf
1 sprig of thyme
salt and pepper

Prepare the vegetables. Slice courgettes, celery, fennel, and leeks; skin onions; leave button mushrooms whole or cut into halves or quarters; dice cucumber or aubergines.

Crush the coriander seeds, skin and crush the garlic, and skin and chop the tomatoes. Put the oil, lemon juice, water, bay leaf, thyme, coriander seeds, garlic, and seasoning into a saucepan. Bring to the boil. Add the tomatoes and cook, uncovered, over moderate heat for 25 minutes. If the vegetables are to be cooked and served hot, add for the appropriate time according to the type of vegetable. If they are already cooked and only need re-heating, or they are to be served raw but hot, add to the sauce for the final 2–3 minutes. If they are to be served cold, pour the hot sauce over the raw vegetables and leave to cool. Remove the bay leaf and thyme before serving.

Note Many different vegetables can be cooked *à la Grecque* and can be served hot or cold. Small portions are often served cold as a first course or as part of a mixed hors d'œuvre. The most usual ones are courgettes, celery, fennel, button onions and mushrooms, and red and green peppers. Cucumber, aubergines, and leeks are also popular.

CELERIAC IN MUSTARD DRESSING

4 helpings

1 medium-sized celeriac
3 × 2.5ml spoons/1½ teaspoons
  salt
3 × 2.5ml spoons/1½ teaspoons
  lemon juice
4 × 15ml spoons/4 tablespoons
  French mustard

3 × 15ml spoons/3 tablespoons
  boiling water
100ml/4 fl oz olive oil *or* as needed
2 × 15ml spoons/2 tablespoons
  white vinegar
salt and pepper

GARNISH

2 × 15ml spoons/2 tablespoons
  chopped mixed herbs *or* parsley

Peel the celeriac, and cut it into matchsticks. Toss the sticks in a bowl with the salt and lemon juice, and leave to stand for 30 minutes. Rinse in a strainer under cold running water, drain well, and pat dry. Put the mustard into a warmed bowl, and very gradually whisk in the boiling water. Then whisk in the oil drop by drop as when making mayonnaise, using enough to make a thick suace. Whisk in the vinegar in the same way. Season with salt and pepper. Fold in the celeriac matchsticks, cover loosely with a cloth, and leave in a cool place for several hours or overnight. Sprinkle the herbs over the dish before serving.

ASPARAGUS WITH HOT LEMON SAUCE

4–8 helpings

50 heads asparagus	25g/1oz butter
250ml/½ pint milk	25g/1oz flour
1 small lettuce	1 egg
1 small onion (75g/3oz approx)	pepper
1 bay leaf	1 × 5ml spoon/1 teaspoon lemon
1 sprig of thyme	juice
salt	8 slices toasted *or* fried bread

GARNISH
chopped parsley	cucumber strips

Prepare the asparagus heads and tie them into bundles. Put the milk into a deep saucepan or asparagus pan. Shred the lettuce finely and skin and chop the onion. Add to the pan with the bay leaf, thyme, and a little salt. Bring the milk to the boil and put in the asparagus. Simmer gently for about 15 minutes or until the asparagus is tender. Remove from the pan and trim off all the inedible parts of the stalks. Untie, and keep the asparagus warm. Strain the milk.

Melt the butter in a small clean saucepan, stir in the flour, and cook gently for 1 minute. Draw off the heat and gradually stir in the strained milk. Return to the heat and stir all the time until the sauce thickens. Cool slightly, beat the egg until liquid, and stir it into the sauce. Season to taste, and add the lemon juice. Arrange the slices of toasted or fried bread on a warmed serving dish, and pile the asparagus on them. Coat with the sauce and garnish with chopped parsley and cucumber strips.

Asparagus with Hot Lemon Sauce

FELAFEL

(Deep-fried Chick-pea Balls)

Makes 36

FELAFEL

200g/7oz cooked chick-peas
75g/3oz fine matzo meal
1 × 5ml spoon/1 teaspoon salt
2 × 5ml spoons/2 teaspoons ground
  cumin

½ × 2.5ml spoon/¼ teaspoon
  ground coriander
½ × 2.5ml spoon/¼ teaspoon
  garlic powder
oil for deep frying

TAHINA SAUCE

50g/2oz ground sesame seeds
75ml/3 fl oz water
½ × 2.5ml spoon/¼ teaspoon
  garlic powder

½ × 2.5ml spoon/¼ teaspoon salt
1 × 15ml spoon/1 tablespoon
  lemon juice
a pinch of pepper

Mince the chick-peas finely or chop and sieve them. Add all the other ingredients for the felafel and form into small balls. Heat the oil to 170–175°C/338–347°F, and fry the felafel until golden-brown.

  For the tahina sauce, mix all ingredients together, and sieve to make a smooth purée, or process in an electric blender for a few minutes. Re-season if required. Serve hot.

CUCUMBER IN SOURED CREAM

4 helpings

3 cucumbers
salt
1 × 5cm/2 inch piece fennel stem
  or 1 thick slice of the bulb
1 hard-boiled egg yolk

pepper
150ml/¼ pint soured cream
1 × 10ml spoon/1 dessertspoon
  cider vinegar *or* white wine
  vinegar

Slice the cucumbers very thinly, sprinkle with the salt; then leave for 30 minutes. Drain and pat dry. Slice the fennel thinly. Crumble the egg yolk coarsely and mix it with the fennel. Just before serving, sprinkle the cucumber with pepper, mix the soured cream with salt and the vinegar, and pour it over the cucumbers. Sprinkle with the fennel and egg.

GARLIC.

HUMMUS

6–8 helpings

300g/11oz cooked chick-peas
150ml/¼ pint tahina (sesame seed paste)
100ml/4 fl oz lemon juice
50ml/2 fl oz cooking liquid from chick-peas, if required

1 clove of garlic
salt
2 × 10ml spoons/2 dessertspoons olive oil
chopped parsley

Grind the chick-peas in a nut-mill, or crush in a pestle and mortar to make a smooth paste. Alternatively, process the chick-peas in an electric blender. In a mixing bowl, blend together the tahina and lemon juice. The mixture should have the consistency of thick cream. If it is too stiff, thin with some of the liquid from cooking the chick-peas. Add the ground chick-peas. Skin and chop the garlic and add to the chick-peas. Stir briskly until well blended. Season with salt. Place the hummus in a shallow serving bowl, trickle the olive oil over it, and sprinkle with chopped parsley.

Serve with French bread, crispbread or pita bread.

Cucumber in Soured Cream

STUFFED TOMATO SALAD

4 helpings

4 large firm tomatoes
salt

lettuce leaves

STUFFING

½ small tomato
3 × 2.5ml spoons/1½ teaspoons
   olive oil
3 × 2.5ml spoons/1½ teaspoons
   chopped onion
3 × 2.5ml spoons/1½ teaspoons
   chopped pimento
½ clove of garlic

3 × 2.5ml spoons/1½ teaspoons
   chopped ham
salt and pepper
2 eggs
2 × 15ml spoons/2 tablespoons
   butter

Cut the tops off the tomatoes, and remove the cores, seeds, and juice with a small spoon, leaving a firm cup of skin and flesh. Keep the tops if desired. (The cores and juice can be sieved for use in a sauce or added to tomato juice.) Sprinkle the tomato cups inside with salt, and turn upside-down on a plate to drain for 30 minutes.

Meanwhile, make the stuffing. Skin, de-seed and chop the tomato. Heat the oil in a saucepan, add the onion and pimento, and simmer, covered, for a few minutes until they soften. Meanwhile, crush the garlic. Add it to the pan with the chopped ham and tomato, and simmer, uncovered, until the liquid has evaporated. Season with salt and pepper and leave to cool. Scramble the eggs in the butter. Leave to cool under buttered paper. When cold, mix with the onion and pimento mixture.

Fill the tomato cups with the stuffing. Remove the stalks from the tops and replace them on the stuffed tomatoes if desired. Serve the tomatoes on a bed of lettuce leaves.

STUFFED AUBERGINES

4 helpings

2 large aubergines
salt
4 × 15ml spoons/4 tablespoons oil

1 × 15ml spoon/1 tablespoon
   grated Parmesan cheese

STUFFING

100g/4oz mushrooms
1 medium-sized onion
1 large tomato
50g/2oz soft white breadcrumbs

1 × 15ml spoon/1 tablespoon
   chopped parsley
pepper

Cut the aubergines in half lengthways. Score the flesh with a knife, sprinkle with salt and leave for 30 minutes for the excess water to drain off. Rinse and dry thoroughly on soft kitchen paper. Brush the aubergines with a little of the oil and cook under a low grill for about 20 minutes or until tender. Remove the aubergine pulp to within 6mm–1.25cm/¼–½ inch of the skin, and chop this finely. Reserve the skins and pulp.

To make the stuffing, clean the mushrooms, skin the onion, and chop both finely. Heat 2 × 15ml spoons/2 tablespoons of the oil in a small saucepan and fry the mushrooms and onion gently for 5 minutes. Skin and chop the tomato. Add to the mushrooms and onion with most of the breadcrumbs, the parsley, aubergine pulp, and seasoning.

Pile the mixture back into the aubergine cases and place in an ovenproof dish. Mix the remaining breadcrumbs with the cheese. Sprinkle this over the stuffing and moisten with the remaining oil. Bake in a fairly hot oven, 200°C/400°F/Gas 6, for 20 minutes.

CRUDITÉS

These are small raw or blanched vegetables, cut up or grated, and served as a first course with an oil and vinegar dressing, French dressing or a dip. They are usually arranged in a decorative pattern on a large flat dish or tray, from which people help themselves. Suitable items to include are:

1) apples (cubed, dipped in lemon juice)
2) black or green olives
3) carrots (cut into matchsticks)
4) cauliflower florets (blanched)
5) celery (raw or blanched, sliced thinly)
6) courgettes (unpeeled, cut into matchsticks)
7) cucumber (cubed or sliced thickly)
8) fennel (raw or blanched, sliced thinly)
9) green or red pepper (cut in rings or strips)
10) radishes (small, whole)
11) spring onions
12) tomatoes (thin wedges, slices, or if small, halved)

SOURED CREAM DIP

3–4 helpings

½ clove of garlic
1 × 15ml spoon/1 tablespoon chilli
  sauce
1 × 5ml spoon/1 teaspoon creamed
  horseradish
1 × 15ml spoon/1 tablespoon
  Worcestershire sauce

½ × 2.5ml spoon/¼ teaspoon dry
  mustard
a pinch of Cayenne pepper
1 × 5ml spoon/1 teaspoon lemon
  juice
250ml/½ pint soured cream

Crush the garlic. In a small basin, combine all the ingredients. Chill for 2–3 hours to allow the flavours to develop.
  Serve with crudités.

Crudités and *Soured Cream Dip*

AUBERGINE PÂTÉ

3–4 helpings

1 large aubergine
1 × 2.5 ml spoon/½ teaspoon salt
a pinch of pepper
1 × 15ml spoon/1 tablespoon
  mayonnaise
1 × 5ml spoon/1 teaspoon lemon
  juice

1 × 5ml spoon/1 teaspoon
  concentrated tomato purée
3 × 2.5ml spoons/1½ teaspoons
  chopped chives *or* spring onions

GARNISH

tomato slices
olives

cucumber slices

Wash and dry the aubergine. Pierce it in several places with a fork. Grill until the skin begins to split and the flesh is soft. Peel the flesh and mash it in a bowl with the other ingredients. Chill, well covered, for a few minutes before serving. Serve on lettuce leaves, on small saucers, garnished with tomato slices, olives, and cucumber slices.

    Eat with thin crackers or rye bread.

EGG-STAND FOR THE BREAKFAST-
TABLE.

EGG & CHEESE DISHES

EGG RÉMOULADE

4 helpings

4 hard-boiled eggs
4 × 15ml spoons/4 tablespoons
  thick mayonnaise

1 × 2.5ml spoon/½ teaspoon
  anchovy essence

GARNISH

tomato
gherkin

4 crisp lettuce leaves

Cut the eggs in half lengthways. Pat dry with kitchen paper. Mix together the mayonnaise and anchovy essence. Turn the eggs, cut side down and coat the white outside with the mayonnaise mixture. Arrange small pieces of tomato or gherkin on top. Place 2 egg halves, cut side down, on each lettuce leaf.

STUFFED EGGS

4 helpings

4 hard-boiled eggs
25g/1oz softened butter
1 × 15ml spoon/1 tablespoon
   mayonnaise

salt and pepper
½ × 15ml spoon/½ tablespoon
   Worcestershire sauce (optional)

GARNISH

parsley sprigs, tomato,
   sliced gherkin, stuffed olives,
   radishes

Cut the eggs in half lengthways. Remove the yolks carefully and press through a fine sieve into a bowl, or mash with a fork. Trim a small slice off the rounded side of each half white so that they stand firmly. Mix the yolks with the butter, mayonnaise, salt, and pepper. Add Worcestershire sauce, if liked. Beat until smooth and creamy, put into a forcing bag with a 1.25cm/½ inch star nozzle and pipe into the egg whites. Garnish with a small piece of parsley or tomato, a slice of gherkin, stuffed olive or a radish.

   Serve on curled lettuce leaves or watercress sprigs.

Aubergine Pâté

POACHED EGGS BELLE HÉLÈNE

—— 6–8 helpings ——

50 heads asparagus	salt
500ml/1 pint milk	50g/2oz butter
1 large lettuce	50g/2oz flour
1 medium-sized onion	7–9 eggs
1 bay leaf	pepper
3 sprigs thyme	1 × 5ml spoon/1 teaspoon lemon juice

Scrape the white stalks of the asparagus and cut off the points. Put the milk into a saucepan and bring to the boil. Shred the lettuce finely and skin and chop the onion. Add to the pan with the bay leaf, thyme, and a little salt; then put in the asparagus stalks. Simmer gently for about 15 minutes or until the stalks are tender. Drain the asparagus, and rub through a fine stainless steel or nylon sieve. Melt the butter in a second pan, add the flour and cook for 1 minute. Remove from the heat and stir in the asparagus purée. Return to the heat and bring to the boil, stirring all the time until the sauce thickens. Beat one of the eggs lightly, stir it into the sauce and continue stirring over very gentle heat, without boiling, until the sauce is very thick. Season the sauce well and add the lemon juice. Cook the asparagus points in boiling salted water for 5 minutes or until tender. Drain well. Poach the eggs and trim neatly to a round shape. Chop the trimmings finely and add them to the sauce. Spoon the sauce in a line down the centre of a heated serving dish. Arrange an equal number of eggs on each side and garnish the top of the sauce, between the eggs, with the asparagus points.

Serve as a first course at dinner.

EGGS IN ASPIC

—— 4 helpings ——

4 eggs	500ml/1 pint liquid aspic jelly

DECORATION

1 or 2 of the following: prawns, shrimps, chervil, tarragon, cress, watercress, cooked peas

GARNISH

cress or watercress sprigs

Poach the eggs in water until the whites are firm and the yolks semi-set. Drain on soft kitchen paper and leave to cool. Trim the eggs with a pastry cutter or sharp knife so they will fit into dariole moulds. Chill the eggs and 4 moulds in the refrigerator. Put a little of the jelly in each mould. Rotate, tilting the mould so that the inside becomes entirely coated with a thin layer of jelly. Chill until set. Arrange a decoration of prawns, leaves or peas on the set jelly, using a long pin or fine skewer to set them in place. Add another layer of jelly carefully. Return to the refrigerator to set. Place 1 egg in each mould and add enough jelly to cover it. Return the moulds and any remaining jelly to the refrigerator. When the jellied eggs are firmly set, turn them out on to a dish. Chop the remaining jelly and arrange round the eggs. Garnish with cress or watercress sprigs.

Note 1 × 15ml spoon/1 tablespoon Madeira or dry sherry can be added to the aspic jelly for an extra rich flavour.

CASED EGGS AND MUSHROOMS

6 helpings

125g/5oz butter
6 medium thick slices white bread
2 sticks celery *or* 1 onion
50g/2oz mushrooms

5 eggs
75ml/3 fl oz milk
salt and pepper
100g/4oz continental sausage

GARNISH

lettuce leaves

watercress sprigs

Melt 100g/4oz of the butter, and let it cool but not solidify. Cut the crusts off the bread. Brush the butter generously on to both sides of each slice so that the bread is saturated, especially at the corners. Press into individual bun tins so that the corners stick upwards, and trim neatly, if necessary. Bake in a fairly hot oven at 200°C/400°F/Gas 6, for 15–20 minutes until golden-brown. Take care that the tips do not brown too much. Leave to cool.

Slice the celery or skin and chop the onion finely. Slice the mushrooms. Melt half the remaining butter in a pan and sauté the celery or onion for 3–4 minutes until softened. Add the mushrooms and cook for 2–3 minutes until tender. Drain.

Beat the eggs, milk, salt, and pepper together lightly. Melt the remaining butter, pour in the beaten egg, reduce the heat and cook gently, stirring all the time, until the mixture is just set and creamy. Cut the sausage into 6mm/¼ inch dice and add to the scrambled egg with the sautéed vegetables. Stir lightly. Leave to cool. Spoon the cold egg into the bread cases.

Serve on lettuce leaves, garnished with small watercress sprigs.

Cased Eggs and Mushrooms

ZÉPHIRE OF CHEESE

4–6 helpings

25g/1oz gelatine
4 × 15ml spoons/4 tablespoons
  cold water
325ml/13 fl oz milk
50g/2oz Cheddar cheese
125ml/¼ pint double cream

50g/2oz grated Parmesan cheese
salt and pepper
a good pinch of grated nutmeg

GARNISH

chopped aspic jelly
watercress sprigs

strips of pimento

Soften the gelatine in the cold water in a small heatproof container. Stand the container in a pan of hot water and stir until the gelatine dissolves. Cool slightly, and mix into the milk. Chill until cold but not set. Meanwhile, grate the Cheddar cheese and whip the cream until semi-stiff. Mix both cheeses, the cream, and seasoning to taste into the cold milk when it is beginning to thicken. Pour the mixture into wetted individual moulds or one 625ml/1¼ pint fluted jelly mould. Chill until set, then turn out, and garnish with the chopped jelly, watercress, and pimento.

CHEESE CREAM

4 helpings

50g/2oz Cheddar *or* Gruyère
  cheese
dry English mustard
a pinch of Cayenne pepper
a pinch of salt

25g/1oz grated Parmesan cheese
4 × 15ml spoons/4 tablespoons
  aspic jelly
125ml/¼ pint double cream

GARNISH

watercress sprigs

Cayenne pepper

Grate the Cheddar or Gruyère cheese very finely. Season it with a little mustard, a pinch of Cayenne pepper, and a good pinch of salt. Mix in the Parmesan cheese. Warm the aspic jelly until just liquid if set; cool it until quite cold but still liquid. Meanwhile, whip the cream until semi-stiff. Stir the liquid aspic jelly into the whipped cream, blending lightly but thoroughly. Fold in the cheeses lightly, a little at a time; do not beat or the mixture will lose its lightness. Turn the mixture into a 375ml/¾ pint glass bowl or individual bowls, and leave to set. When cold, garnish with watercress sprigs which have been dusted lightly with Cayenne pepper.

CHEESE PÂTÉ

125g/5oz Roquefort *or* other blue cheese
125g/5oz full-fat soft cheese
1 × 15ml spoon/1 tablespoon softened butter
125g/5oz Cheddar cheese
75g/3oz walnuts

1 × 2.5ml spoon/½ teaspoon Worcestershire sauce
1 × 2.5ml spoon/½ teaspoon paprika
a pinch of Cayenne pepper
chopped parsley

Crumble the blue cheese. Blend together with the soft cheese and butter with the back of a spoon. Grate the Cheddar cheese finely and work it in. Chop the walnuts finely. Add them to the mixture with the Worcestershire sauce, paprika, and Cayenne pepper and mix well. Shape the cheese mixture into a ball. Roll in enough parsley to cover completely. Cover with clingfilm and chill.

Serve in small wedges on lettuce leaves, with slices of toast or pumpernickel.

Cheese Pâté

CAMEMBERT OR BRIE SOUFFLÉ

— 4 helpings —

100g/4oz ripe Camembert *or* Brie cheese
100g/4oz cottage *or* curd cheese
1 × 10ml spoon/1 dessertspoon gelatine

125ml/¼ pint whole *or* skimmed milk
salt
2 egg whites

Cut the crusts off the Camembert or Brie cheese. Sieve or mash with the cottage or curd cheese until both are smooth and well-blended. Soften the gelatine in the milk in a small heatproof container. Stand in very hot water, and stir until the gelatine dissolves. Leave to cool, then mix with the cheeses and seasoning. Chill. Whisk the egg whites until stiff but not dry. When the cheese mixture is beginning to set at the edges, fold in the egg whites lightly but thoroughly. turn into a wetted 500ml/1 pint soufflé dish, and chill until set.

MACE.

CHEESE RAMEKINS

— 4 helpings —

25g/1oz Cheshire cheese
50ml/2 fl oz milk (approx)
25g/1oz soft white breadcrumbs (approx)
25g/1oz grated Parmesan cheese

25g/1oz softened unsalted butter
1 egg
salt and pepper
a pinch of ground mace
butter for greasing

Grate the Cheshire cheese finely. Heat the milk and pour just enough over the breadcrumbs to cover them. Leave to stand for 5–10 minutes. Stir in both cheeses and the butter. Separate the egg, and mix the yolk into the cheese mixture. Season well with salt, pepper and mace. Whisk the egg white until very stiff. Stir one spoonful into the cheese mixture, then fold in the rest. Turn the mixture gently into 4 small greased ovenproof pots or ramekins. Bake in a fairly hot oven at 200°C/400°F/Gas 6, for 15–20 minutes, or until risen and slightly browned. Serve as soon as possible before they sink.

Opposite, from the top clockwise:
Zéphire of Cheese (page 30),
Cheese Ramekins (page 32) and
Eggs in Aspic (page 28)

FISH & SHELLFISH DISHES

SMOKED SALMON

Slice the salmon very thinly and serve with lemon wedges, Cayenne pepper, and brown bread and butter. Alternatively, form thicker slices into cornets and secure with cocktail sticks, if necessary.

TARAMASALATA

4 helpings

100g/4oz smoked cod's roe
1 clove of garlic
2 × 15ml spoons/2 tablespoons
   lemon juice
4 × 15ml spoons/4 tablespoons
   olive oil

2 × 15ml spoons/2 tablespoons
   cold water
freshly ground black pepper

Skin the roe and garlic. Pound them in a mortar with the lemon juice until smooth. Add small amounts of oil and water alternately until the mixture is completely blended. Season to taste with black pepper, and serve with pita bread.

MRS BEETON'S DRESSED WHITEBAIT

3–4 helpings

50g/2oz flour
salt and pepper
100g/4oz whitebait

milk
fat for deep frying
Cayenne pepper

GARNISH

parsley sprigs

lemon wedges

Season the flour with salt and pepper. Wash the whitebait, dip in milk, and coat with flour, by shaking them together in a tea-towel or plastic bag. Make sure that the fish are separate. Heat the fat to 190–195°C/375–383°F, and fry the fish in small batches until crisp. Check that the fat is at the correct temperature before putting in each batch. When all the fish are fried, sprinkle with salt and Cayenne pepper. Serve immediately, garnished with parsley and lemon wedges, with thinly cut brown bread and butter.

Note Whitebait are eaten whole.

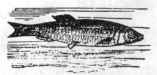

THE HERRING.

HERRING ROLLS

4 helpings

4 salted *or* rollmop herrings	25g/1 oz butter
2 hard-boiled eggs	Cayenne pepper
8 anchovy fillets	lemon juice

GARNISH

8 lemon slices	1 small diced beetroot
4–6 sliced gherkins	chopped parsley

If using salted herrings, soak them in cold water for several hours, then fillet, and remove all the bones. If using rollmop herrings, divide each into 2 fillets. Separate the egg yolks and whites. Chop the anchovy fillets and egg yolks finely, and mix them with the butter and pepper. Spread most of the anchovy mixture on the herring fillets and roll up firmly. Spread the remaining mixture thinly on the round ends of each roll. Chop the egg whites finely and use to coat the spread end of the rolls. Sprinkle the rolls with a little lemon juice and garnish with lemon slices, gherkins, beetroot, and parsley.

Smoked Salmon

CUCUMBER CASSOLETTES

4 helpings

1 large *or* 2 thin cucumbers
olive oil
vinegar
salt and pepper
200g/7oz crabmeat *or* cooked *or*
   canned red salmon

3 × 15ml spoons/3 tablespoons
   mayonnaise
Tabasco sauce
65g/2½oz canned anchovy fillets

GARNISH

chopped parsley

Peel the cucumbers and cut them into 5cm/2 inch thick pieces. Remove the seeds with an apple corer or potato peeler. Place the rings on a dish and pour a little oil and vinegar over them; season well. Pound the crabmeat or salmon and mix it with the mayonnaise and a few drops of Tabasco sauce. Drain the cucumber pieces and fill the centres with the fish mixture. Drain the anchovy fillets and twist one round the top of each cucumber ring. Garnish with parsley. Serve on small round croûtes or biscuits if desired.

PRAWN COCKTAIL

4 helpings

4 lettuce leaves
200g/7oz peeled prawns
5 × 15ml spoons/5 tablespoons
   mayonnaise
1 × 15ml spoon/1 tablespoon
   concentrated tomato purée *or*
   tomato ketchup

a pinch of Cayenne pepper *or* a few
   drops Tabasco sauce
salt (optional)
1 × 5ml spoon/1 teaspoon vinegar
   or tarragon vinegar (optional)

GARNISH

4 shell-on prawns

Shred the lettuce leaves. Place a little shredded lettuce at the bottom of 4 glass dishes. Put the prawns on top. Mix the mayonnaise with the tomato purée or ketchup and add a pinch of Cayenne pepper or a few drops of Tabasco sauce. Season with salt and vinegar if required. Pour the mayonnaise over the prawns and garnish each dish with an unshelled prawn.

   Serve with rolled brown bread and butter.

THE PRAWN.

SPANISH PRAWNS

5–6 helpings

75ml/3 fl oz cooking oil
1 clove of garlic
a small bunch of chives
500g/1lb cooked shell-on prawns

2 × 15ml spoons/2 tablespoons dry
   sherry
salt and black pepper

Pour the oil into a large flat pan, and heat for a few minutes. Crush the garlic, chop the chives, and add to the oil. Put the prawns (with the shells) in the pan with the sherry. Season with salt and black pepper. Cover the pan and cook for 5 minutes, turning the prawns once.

   Serve in small bowls, with crusty French bread. Hand paper napkins and fingerbowls separately.

Spanish Prawns

MEAT DISHES

PROSCIUTTO CON FICHI

(Smoked Ham with Fresh Figs)

4 helpings

250g/8oz Parma ham
salad oil
4 large lettuce leaves

250g/8oz fresh figs
8 black olives

The ham should be cut in paper-thin slices. Brush each slice lightly with a little oil and place on the lettuce leaves. Cut a cross in the top of each fig, and open the points out slightly, to imitate the petals of a flower. Arrange the black olives alternately with the figs on the ham.

ONION.

HAM RAMEKINS

8 helpings

225g/8oz lean cooked ham
2 eggs
4 × 15ml spoons/4 tablespoons milk
½ × 5ml spoon/½ teaspoon dried mixed herbs

½ × 2.5ml spoon/¼ teaspoon dry mustard
salt and pepper
fat for greasing
paprika

Chop the ham finely. Separate the eggs. Whisk the egg yolks lightly, add the ham, milk, herbs, mustard, salt and pepper, and mix together well. Divide the mixture equally between 8 well-greased ramekin dishes, filling each about three-quarters full. Cook in a fairly hot oven at 190°C/375°F/Gas 5, for 15 minutes until set. Meanwhile, whisk the egg whites until stiff, and add a little salt. Divide the meringue between the dishes, piling it up roughly. Sprinkle with paprika, return the dishes to the oven, and bake them for another 10–15 minutes until crisp and lightly browned. Serve at once.

CHOPPED LIVER

4–5 helpings

1 medium-sized onion
225g/8oz chicken *or* calf's liver
4 × 10ml spoons/4 dessertspoons
   chicken fat

2 hard-boiled eggs
salt and freshly ground pepper

GARNISH

lettuce leaves

tomato slices

Skin and chop the onion. Remove any gristle or tubes from the liver. Heat the chicken fat in a frying pan. Fry the onion with the liver until soft but not brown. Mince the liver, onion, and hard-boiled eggs very finely. Season with salt and freshly ground pepper, and mix to a paste.

   Serve on a bed of lettuce leaves, garnished with tomato slices.

Prosciutto Con Fichi

LIVER PÂTÉ WITH MUSHROOMS

Makes 2.25kg/4¹/₂lb (approx)

1kg/2lb lamb's *or* pig's liver
1kg/2lb green bacon, without rinds
1 × 5ml spoon/1 teaspoon salt
freshly ground pepper
a pinch of ground cinnamon *or*
   grated nutmeg

1 small onion
125g/4oz small cup mushrooms
125g/4oz butter *or* margarine
2 eggs
a pinch of dried thyme

GARNISH

3 bay leaves

Remove any skin and tubes from the liver. Chop the bacon. Mince together finely or process in an electric blender. Add the salt, pepper, and cinnamon or nutmeg. Skin the onion and chop it finely; clean and slice the mushrooms. Melt the butter or margarine in a pan and fry the onion and mushrooms gently for 4–5 minutes, turning frequently. Remove from the heat and stir in the liver and bacon. Beat the eggs lightly until liquid and stir them into the mixture.

Put the mixture into a shallow ovenproof casserole or dish with a lid. Sprinkle the surface with thyme and put the bay leaves in a trefoil pattern on top. Cover the dish and stand it in a pan of hot water which comes half-way up the sides. Bake in a cool oven, 150°C/300°F/Gas 2, for 3 hours. When cooked, leave to cool, keeping the lid on the dish. Chill before serving from the dish.

SOUPS

—— • ——

The principal art in composing good rich soup, is so to proportion the several ingredients that the flavour of one shall not predominate over another, and that all the articles of which it is composed, shall form an agreeable whole. To accomplish this, care must be taken that the roots and herbs are perfectly well cleaned, and that the water is proportioned to the quantity of meat and other ingredients.

Isabella Beeton 1861

Top: *Hollandaise Soup (page 63)*
Bottom: *Jellied Tomato Soup
with Soured Cream (page 68)*

STOCKS

BROWN STOCK

(Beef stock)

Makes 1.5 litres/3 pints (approx)

500g/1 lb beef *or* veal marrow
  bones
500g/1 lb lean shin of beef
1.5 litres/3 pints cold water
1 × 5ml spoon/1 teaspoon salt
1 medium-sized onion

1 medium-sized carrot
1 stick of celery
bouquet garni
1 × 2.5ml spoon/½ teaspoon black
  peppercorns

Ask the butcher to chop the bones into manageable pieces. Wipe them thoroughly. Trim off any fat and cut the meat into small pieces. Put the bones and meat in a roasting tin in a hot oven at 220°C/425°F/Gas 7, for 30-40 minutes to brown, turning them occasionally.

Put the browned bones and meat in a large saucepan with the water and salt. Prepare and slice the vegetables. Add them to the pan with the bouquet garni and peppercorns. Heat slowly to boiling point, skim well, and cover the pan with a tight-fitting lid. Reduce the heat and simmer very gently for 4 hours. Strain through a fine sieve and leave to cool. When cold, remove any fat from the surface.

GENERAL HOUSEHOLD STOCK

Makes 1 litre/2 pints (approx)

1kg/2 lb cooked *or* raw bones of any
  meat *or* poultry, cooked *or* raw
  meat trimmings, giblets, and
  bacon rinds
500g/1 lb onions, carrots, celery,
  and leeks

salt
1 bay leaf
4 black peppercorns

Break or chop the bones into manageable pieces. Wipe thoroughly. Prepare and slice the vegetables, retaining a piece of brown onion skin if a brown stock is required. Put the bones and meat trimmings into a saucepan. Cover with cold water and add 1 × 2.5ml spoon/½ teaspoon salt for each litre/2 pints of water used. Heat slowly to simmering point. Add the other ingredients. Simmer, uncovered, for at least 3 hours. Strain and cool quickly by standing the pan in chilled water. When cold, skim off the fat. If the stock is not required at once, keep it cold. Use within 24 hours, or within 3 days if kept in a refrigerator. Reboil before use.

STEWPAN.

WHITE STOCK

Makes 2 litres/4 pints (approx)

1kg/2 lb knuckle of veal
1 medium-sized onion
1 stick of celery
2 litres/4 pints cold water
1 × 10ml spoon/1 dessertspoon salt

1 × 10ml spoon/1 dessertspoon
  white vinegar *or* lemon juice
1 × 2.5ml spoon/½ teaspoon white
  peppercorns
a small strip of lemon rind
1 bay leaf

Chop the knuckle into manageable pieces. Scrape the bones, trim off any fat, and wipe the bones thoroughly. Prepare and slice the onion and celery. Put the bones in a large pan with the cold water, salt, and vinegar or lemon juice. Heat to boiling point and skim. Add the vegetables and the other ingredients. Bring back to the boil, cover, reduce the heat, and simmer gently for 4 hours. Strain the stock through a fine sieve and cool it quickly by standing the pan in chilled water. When cold, skim off the fat. Store as for General Household Stock (page 8).

Brown Stock

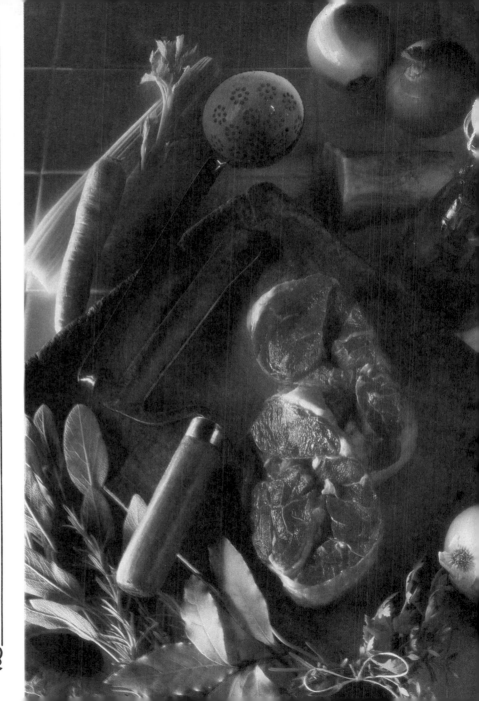

FISH STOCK

Makes 1 litre/2 pints (using 1 litre/2 pints water)

bones, skin, and heads from
    filleted fish *or* fish trimmings *or*
    cod's *or* other fish heads *or* any
    mixture of these
1 × 5ml spoon/1 teaspoon salt

1 small onion
1 stick of celery
4 white peppercorns
bouquet garni

Break up the bones and wash the fish trimmings, if used. Prepare and slice the vegetables. Put the bones, fish trimmings, or heads in a saucepan and cover with cold water. Add the salt. Heat to boiling point. Add the vegetables, the peppercorns, and bouquet garni. Cover, and simmer gently for 40 minutes. Strain the stock through a fine sieve.

Note If cooked for longer than 40 minutes, fish stock tastes bitter. It does not keep unless frozen, and should be made only as required.

COURT BOUILLON

(for salmon, salmon trout, and other whole fish)

water
500ml/1 pint dry white wine *or* dry
    cider to each litre/2 pints water
2 × 15ml spoons/2 tablespoons
    white wine vinegar to each litre/2
    pints water
2 large carrots

2 large onions
2–3 sticks celery
parsley stalks
1 bouquet garni to each litre/2 pints
    water
a few peppercorns
salt and pepper

Put the liquids in a large pan. Slice the carrots and onions, chop the celery, and crush the parsley stalks. Add to the liquid with the remaining ingredients. Simmer for 30 minutes, leave to cool, then strain and use as required.

VEGETABLE STOCK

Makes 2 litres/4 pints (approx)

2 large carrots
2 medium-sized onions
3 sticks celery
2 tomatoes
25g/1oz butter *or* margarine
2 litres/4 pints boiling water

1 × 2.5ml spoon/½ teaspoon yeast
    extract
bouquet garni
1 × 5ml spoon/1 teaspoon salt
6 black peppercorns
a blade of mace
outer leaves of 1 lettuce *or* ¼ small
    cabbage

Slice the carrots, onions, and celery thinly and chop the tomatoes. Melt the fat in a large saucepan and fry the carrots, onions, and celery for 5–10 minutes until the onions are golden-brown. Add the tomatoes and fry for a further minute. Add the water and the rest of the ingredients, except the lettuce or cabbage. Cover, and simmer for 1 hour. Shred the lettuce or cabbage, and add to the pan. Simmer for a further 20 minutes. Strain through a fine sieve. Use the same day, if possible, or cool quickly and store in a refrigerator for up to 2 days.

CARROTS.

CHICKEN STOCK

Makes 1 litre/2 pints (using 1 litre/2 pints water)

1 medium-sized onion
1 stick of celery
carcass of 1 chicken *or* game bird,
   including the giblets

cleaned feet of bird (optional)
1 × 10ml spoon/1 dessertspoon salt
4 white peppercorns
bouquet garni

Prepare and slice the vegetables. Break or chop the carcass into manageable pieces. Put the carcass, giblets, and feet, if used, in a large saucepan, cover with cold water, and add the salt. Heat to boiling point. Draw the pan off the heat and leave to stand for 2–3 minutes, then skim off any fat. Add the vegetables, peppercorns, and bouquet garni. Re-heat to boiling point, cover, reduce the heat, and simmer very gently for 3–4 hours. Strain the stock through a fine sieve and cool it quickly by standing the container in chilled water. When cold, skim off the fat. Store as for General Household Stock (page 8).

Chicken Stock

THIN SOUPS & CONSOMMÉS

CHICKEN BROTH

8 helpings

1 small boiling fowl (1.5kg/3 lb approx) or 1 chicken carcass with some flesh left on it
giblets of the bird
1.5–2 litres/3–4 pints water
1 × 5ml spoon/1 teaspoon salt
1 medium-sized onion
2 medium-sized carrots

1 stick of celery
½ × 2.5ml spoon/¼ teaspoon ground pepper
a blade of mace
bouquet garni
a strip of lemon rind
25g/1oz long-grain rice (optional)
1 × 15ml spoon/1 tablespoon chopped parsley

Joint the boiling fowl or break up the carcass bones, and wash the giblets. Put them into a large saucepan and cover with the cold water. Add the salt, and heat slowly to simmering point. Cut the onion in half, and dice the carrots and celery. Add the vegetables to the pan with the pepper, mace, bouquet garni, and lemon rind. Cover, and simmer gently for 3–3½ hours if using a raw boiling fowl, or for 1½ hours if using a chicken carcass. Strain the broth through a colander. Skim off the fat.

Return the broth to the pan and re-heat to simmering point. Wash the rice, if used, and sprinkle it into the broth. Cover, and simmer for a further 15–20 minutes until the rice is cooked.

Some of the meat can be chopped finely and added to the broth, the rest can be used in made-up dishes, eg a fricassée. Just before serving the broth, re-season if required, and add the chopped parsley.

Overleaf
From the top, clockwise
Green Herb Consommé (page 24), Scots Broth (above) and
Consommé Brunoise (page 21)

SPRING BROTH

4–6 helpings

12 spring onions
4 young carrots
1 small turnip
a few heads sprue asparagus
100g/4oz shelled green peas
2 × 10ml spoons/2 dessertspoons olive oil or butter

1 litre/2 pints white stock (page 9) or general household stock (page 8)
salt and pepper
1 × 10ml spoon/1 dessertspoon chopped parsley

Cut the spring onions and carrots into thin rings and the turnip into 6mm/¼ inch dice. Remove the tips of the asparagus and reserve. Cut the tender parts of the stalks into 6mm/¼ inch lengths. Heat the oil or butter in a pan, add all the vegetables, cover, and cook over gentle heat for about 10 minutes. Do not let them brown. Heat the stock to boiling point, add to the pan, cover, and simmer gently for 30 minutes. Add the asparagus tips, cover, and simmer for a further 15 minutes. Season to taste, and add the chopped parsley just before serving.

Scots or Scotch Broth

500g/1lb scrag end of neck of
   mutton
1 × 5ml spoon/1 teaspoon salt
1 litre/2 pints cold water
50g/2oz pearl barley
2 medium carrots

2 leeks
1 small turnip
1 stick of celery
pepper
1 × 10ml spoon/1 dessertspoon
   chopped parsley

Wipe and trim the meat, and cut into 2.5cm/1 inch pieces. Put into
a deep pan with the bones, salt, and cold water. Heat gently to
simmering point. Blanch the barley. Add to the pan, cover and
simmer gently for 2 hours. Prepare the vegetables, setting aside
one whole carrot and cutting the rest into 6mm/¼ inch dice. Add
them to the broth, cover, and simmer for another hour. Grate the
whole carrot and add it to the broth 20 minutes before serving.
Skim the fat. Remove the bones. Season to taste with pepper and
add the chopped parsley just before serving.

Chicken Broth

HOTCH POTCH

1kg/2lb scrag and middle neck of
    lamb *or* mutton
1.25 litres/2½ pints water
1 × 10ml spoon/1 dessertspoon salt
bouquet garni
1 medium-sized carrot
1 small turnip
6 spring onions

1 small lettuce
100g/4oz shelled young broad
    beans *or* runner beans
100g/4oz cauliflower florets
150g/5oz shelled peas
salt and pepper
1 × 15ml spoon/1 tablespoon
    chopped parsley

Wipe the meat and trim off any excess fat. Remove the meat from the bone and cut the meat into small pieces. Put the bone and meat into a large saucepan, add the water, and heat very slowly to simmering point. Add the salt and the bouquet garni, cover, and simmer very gently for 30 minutes.

Meanwhile, cut the carrot and turnip into 6mm/¼ inch dice and the spring onions into thin rings; shred the lettuce and runner beans, if used. Add the carrot, turnip, and spring onions to the pan, cover, and simmer for 1½ hours. Add the rest of the vegetables to the soup, cover, and simmer for a further 30 minutes. Season to taste. Skim off the fat and remove the bouquet garni and the bones. Add the chopped parsley just before serving.

Note The vegetables can be varied according to the season.

Opposite, from the top clockwise:
*Green Herb Consommé (page 51),
Scots Broth (page 47)* and *Consommé
Brunoise (page 49)*

CONSOMMÉ BRUNOISE

1 × 2.5ml spoon/½ teaspoon
    lemon juice
1 × 15ml spoon/1 tablespoon
    sherry (optional)
1 × 15ml spoon/1 tablespoon finely
    diced carrot

1 × 15ml spoon/1 tablespoon finely
    diced turnip
1 × 15ml spoon/1 tablespoon finely
    diced greek leek
1 × 15ml spoon/1 tablespoon finely
    diced celery

CONSOMMÉ

100g/4oz lean shin of beef
125ml/¼ pint water
1 small onion
1 small carrot
1 small stick of celery

1.25 litres/2½ pints cold brown
    stock (page 6)
bouquet garni
½ × 2.5ml spoon/¼ teaspoon salt
4 white peppercorns
white and crushed shell of 1 egg

Make the consommé first. Shred the beef finely, trimming off all the fat. Soak the meat in the water for 15 minutes. Prepare the vegetables. Put the meat, water, and the rest of the ingredients into a deep saucepan adding the egg white and shell last. Heat slowly to simmering point, whisking all the time, until a froth rises to the surface. Remove the whisk, cover, and simmer the consommé very gently for 1½–2 hours. Do not allow to boil or the froth will break up and cloud the consommé. Strain slowly into a basin through muslin or a scalded jelly bag. If necessary, strain the consommé again.

Re-heat the consommé to boiling point, and add the lemon juice and sherry, if used. Cook the diced vegetables very carefully in boiling salted water until just tender. Drain and rinse the vegetables; then put them into a warmed tureen.

Pour the hot consommé over the diced vegetables, and serve.

Note This recipe makes 1 litre/2 pints consommé.

CLEAR TOMATO SOUP

4–6 helpings

2 medium-sized tomatoes

orange *or* lemon slices

1 litre/2 pints consommé (page 21)
white and crushed shell of 1 egg

GARNISH (optional)

1 × 15ml spoon/1 tablespoon each
of diced carrot, celery, and green
leek

Skin the tomatoes and cut them into small pieces. Add to the consommé, heat to simmering point, and simmer for 10 minutes. Strain the consommé, then return it to the pan. Add the egg white and shell, re-heat slowly to simmering point, whisking all the time, until a froth rises to the surface. Strain slowly into a basin through muslin or a scalded jelly bag; if necessary, strain again.

Garnish, if liked, with orange or lemon slices. Alternatively, cook the diced vegetables separately in boiling salted water until tender. Drain and put in a warmed tureen. Re-heat the consommé and pour over them.

THE NUTMEG.

GREEN HERB CONSOMMÉ

6 helpings

2 medium-sized tomatoes
1 litre/2 pints white stock (page 9)
  or chicken stock (page 10)
a bunch of fresh mixed herbs
  (marjoram, basil, thyme)

white and crushed shell of 1 egg
1 × 2.5ml spoon/½ teaspoon
  lemon juice
50ml/2 fl oz dry white wine
  (optional)

GARNISH

1 × 15ml spoon/1 tablespoon
  shredded lettuce leaves
1 × 15ml spoon/1 tablespoon
  shredded spinach *or* sorrel leaves
1 × 15ml spoon/1 tablespoon small
  green peas

1 × 10ml spoon/1 dessertspoon
  shredded cucumber rind
extra white stock
6 mint leaves
6 chives
6 chervil leaves

Skin the tomatoes and dice the flesh. Heat the stock to boiling point and add the tomatoes and herbs. Add the white and shell and heat slowly to simmering point, whisking all the time, until a froth rises to the surface. Remove the whisk, cover, and simmer very gently for 30 minutes only. Strain slowly into a basin through muslin or a scalded jelly bag.

Meanwhile, cook the vegetables for the garnish separately in a little boiling stock until just tender. Chop the mint and the chives.

Heat the consommé to boiling point and add the cooked vegetables for the garnish with the stock in which they were cooked. Re-heat for 1 minute only. Just before serving, add the lemon juice, wine, if used, and chopped mint and chives. Float 1 chervil leaf on top of each helping.

THICK SOUPS

CREAM OF CHICKEN SOUP

4–6 helpings

25g/1oz cornflour
125ml/¼ pint milk
1 litre/2 pints chicken stock (page 10)
50g/2oz cooked chicken
salt and pepper
1 × 5ml spoon/1 teaspoon lemon juice
a pinch of grated nutmeg
2 egg yolks
2 × 15ml spoons/2 tablespoons single cream

Blend the cornflour with a little of the milk. Heat the stock to boiling point and stir into the blended cornflour. Return the mixture to the pan and re-heat to boiling point, stirring all the time. Reduce the heat, cover, and simmer for 20 minutes. Cut the chicken into 6mm/¼ inch dice and heat these in the soup. Season to taste, and add the lemon juice and nutmeg. Beat the yolks with the rest of the milk and the cream; beat in a little hot soup, and fold into the rest of the soup. Heat until it thickens, but do not allow it to boil.

Clear Tomato Soup

BROWN WINDSOR SOUP

6 helpings

150g/5oz shin of beef
150g/5oz stewing lamb
1 medium-sized onion
1 carrot
35g/1½oz butter
35g/1½oz flour
1.75 litres/3½ pints beef stock *or*
  strong general household stock
  (page 8)

bouquet garni
salt
a few grains Cayenne pepper
75ml/3fl oz brown sherry *or*
  Madeira (optional)
35g/1½oz boiled rice (optional)

GARNISH

toasted croûtons

Cut the beef and lamb into 2.5cm/1 inch pieces. Skin and slice the onion, and slice the carrot. Heat the butter in a deep heavy saucepan, put in the meat and vegetables, and fry gently until lightly browned. Stir in the flour, and continue cooking until it is well browned. Add the stock gradually, stirring all the time. Heat to boiling point, add the bouquet garni, cover, reduce the heat, and simmer for 2 hours or until the meat is very tender. Season to taste with salt and Cayenne pepper.

Strain the soup into a clean pan. Discard the bouquet garni, and remove any bones, skin and gristle from the meat. Return the meat to the soup, and either rub through a sieve or process in an electric blender to obtain a smooth purée. Return the purée to the pan, add the sherry or Madeira if used, and re-season if required. Just before serving, add the rice if used, and re-heat throroughly. Serve garnished with croûtons.

MULLIGATAWNY SOUP

4 helpings

400g/13oz lean mutton, rabbit,
  stewing veal *or* shin of beef
1 medium-sized onion
1 small cooking apple
25g/1oz butter *or* margarine
2 × 15ml spoons/2 tablespoons
  curry powder
25g/1oz plain flour
1 litre/2 pints water

1 large carrot
½ small parsnip
bouquet garni
1 × 2.5ml spoon/½ teaspoon
  lemon juice
1 × 2.5ml spoon/½ teaspoon salt
½ × 2.5ml spoon/¼ teaspoon
  black treacle *or* extra lemon juice

Trim off any fat and cut the meat into small pieces. Prepare the onion and apple and chop them finely. Melt the fat in a deep saucepan and fry the onion and apple quickly for 2–3 minutes. Add the curry powder, cook gently for 2 minutes, then stir in the flour. Gradually add the water and stir until boiling. Add the meat. Prepare and slice the carrot and parsnip, and add to the pan with the bouquet garni, lemon juice, and salt. Simmer until the meat is very tender. This will take 2 hours for rabbit, 3 hours for stewing veal and mutton, and 4 hours for shin of beef.

Taste the soup, and add black treacle or more lemon juice to obtain a flavour that is neither predominantly sweet nor acid. Strain the soup. Dice some of the meat finely, add to the soup and re-heat.

Serve with boiled long-grain rice.

Note The amount of curry powder can be varied to taste; the quantity given above is for a mild-flavoured soup.

COCK-A-LEEKIE

8 helpings

100g/4oz prunes
1 small boiling fowl with giblets
   (1.5kg/3lb approx)
3 rashers streaky bacon, without
   rinds (optional)
1kg/2lb veal *or* beef marrow bones
   (optional)

500g/1lb leeks
1.5–2 litres/3–4 pints cold water
2 × 5ml spoons/2 teaspoons salt
½ × 2.5ml spoon/¼ teaspoon
   pepper
bouquet garni

Soak the prunes overnight in cold water; then stone them. Wipe the fowl and wash the giblets. Chop the bacon, if used. Chop the bones into manageable pieces, if used. Wash and trim the leeks and cut them into thin rings. Put the fowl, giblets, marrow bones, and bacon into a deep pan, cover with cold water, add the salt, and heat very slowly to simmering point. Reserve 4 × 15ml spoons/4 tablespoons of the leeks and add the remaining leeks, the pepper, and bouquet garni to the pan. Cover, and simmer gently for about 3 hours, or until the fowl is tender.

Remove the fowl, carve off the meat and cut it into fairly large serving pieces. Strain the liquid. Return the pieces to the soup with the soaked and stoned prunes and the remaining sliced leeks. Simmer very gently for 30 minutes until the prunes are just tender but not broken. Re-season if required, and serve the soup with the prunes.

Cock-a-Leekie

OXTAIL SOUP

4–6 helpings

1 oxtail
25g/1oz beef dripping
1 medium-sized onion
1 large carrot
1 turnip
1 stick of celery

1 litre/2 pints water *or* general
 household stock (page 8)
1 × 5ml spoon/1 teaspoon salt
bouquet garni
6 black peppercorns
25g/1oz plain flour

Wash, trim off any fat, and joint the tail. Heat the dripping in a saucepan. Add half the jointed tail and fry until the meat is browned. Lift out the meat and reserve the fat in the pan. Prepare and slice the vegetables. Fry in the hot dripping until golden-brown, then remove. Put all the oxtail and the fried vegetables into a deep saucepan. Add the water or stock, and heat very slowly to boiling point. Add the salt, bouquet garni, and peppercorns. Cover, and simmer very gently for 3–4 hours.

Meanwhile, stir the flour into the dripping in the saucepan and fry gently until golden-brown. Strain the soup. Remove all the meat from the bones. Return some of the smaller pieces of meat and any small slices of carrot to the soup. Whisk in the browned flour. Re-heat the soup to boiling point, whisking all the time. Re-season if required.

FISHERMAN'S HOT POT

4 helpings

50g/2oz white cabbage
100g/4oz leek
250g/8oz potatoes
100g/4oz onions
25g/1oz red pepper
2 slices white bread
50ml/2fl oz cooking oil
25g/1oz butter
250g/8oz cod *or* other white fish
 fillets (see **Note**)

150ml/6fl oz Muscadet *or* other dry
 white wine
1 litre/2 pints water
50g/2oz concentrated tomato purée
1 chicken stock cube
bouquet garni
1 clove of garlic
salt and pepper

GARNISH

1 × 15ml spoon/1 tablespoon
 chopped parsley

Shred the cabbage, slice the leek and potatoes, chop the onion and pepper. Remove the crusts from the bread, cut into 1.25cm/½ inch cubes, and dry in the oven for 10 minutes.

Heat the oil and butter in a large saucepan, add the vegetables, cover, and cook gently for 7–8 minutes; do not let them colour. Skin the fish, cut them into 2.5cm/1 inch cubes, and fry for 3 minutes with the vegetables, turning them over to firm the surface of the cubes. Pour in the wine, water, and tomato purée. Crumble in the stock cube. Skin and crush the garlic. Add the bouquet garni and garlic, and season to taste. Heat to simmering point and simmer for 20 minutes. Discard the bouquet garni. Pour into a soup tureen and sprinkle with the chopped parsley.

Note Any white fish can be used for the hot pot, eg haddock, hake, whiting, ling, etc.

HADDOCK, COD OR SKATE SOUP

4–6 helpings

625g/1¼lb haddock, cod, skate *or* any available white fish
2 large onions
1 large carrot
2 sticks celery
200g/7oz potatoes
25g/1oz butter
2 × 10ml spoons/2 dessertspoons olive oil

1 × 5ml spoon/1 teaspoon curry powder
750ml/1½ pints boiling water
bouquet garni
salt and pepper
50ml/2fl oz white wine (optional)
25g/1oz flour
125ml/¼ pint milk
75ml/3fl oz single cream

Prepare the fish and cut them into small pieces. Prepare the onions, carrot, and celery and slice thinly. Peel and dice the potatoes. Heat the butter and olive oil in a deep saucepan. Add all the vegetables and fry gently for 10 minutes. Stir in the curry powder and cook for 3 minutes. Add the boiling water, bouquet garni, and seasoning to taste. Add the fish and re-heat the soup to simmering point; cover, and simmer until the fish is tender.

Transfer the best pieces of fish from the soup and keep them hot in a little of the liquid. Simmer the rest of the soup, uncovered, for 15 minutes until it is reduced. Remove the bouquet garni and rub the soup through a sieve, or process in an electric blender. Add the wine, if used, and re-heat the soup. Blend the flour with a little of the cold milk and then stir in the rest of the milk. Stir it into the soup and heat to boiling point. Add the pieces of fish and the cream to the soup at boiling point, but do not reboil.

Oxtail Soup

LOBSTER BISQUE

4–6 helpings

shell, trimmings, and a little of the flesh of a small *or* medium-sized lobster
1 medium-sized onion
1 medium-sized carrot
1 clove of garlic
1 bay leaf
a blade of mace
1 × 5ml spoon/1 teaspoon lemon juice
1 × 5ml spoon/1 teaspoon anchovy essence
125ml/¼ pint white wine
750ml/1½ pints fish stock (page 12)
salt
1 × 15ml spoon/1 tablespoon cooked lobster coral
50g/2oz butter
25g/1oz flour
125ml/¼ pint single cream
pepper
a few drops red food colouring (optional)

Crush the lobster shell. Flake the rough pieces of flesh finely, keeping the neat pieces for a garnish. Prepare the onion, carrot, and garlic and slice them thinly. Put the shell, flaked lobster, vegetables, bay leaf, mace, lemon juice, anchovy essence, and wine into a deep saucepan. Heat quickly to boiling point and cook briskly for 3–5 minutes. The alcohol in the wine extracts much of the flavour from the lobster and vegetables. Add the fish stock and a little salt. Heat to boiling point, cover, reduce the heat, and simmer for 1 hour.

Strain the soup through a metal sieve and rub through any pieces of firm lobster. Pound the lobster coral with half the butter and rub through a sieve. Melt the rest of the butter in a saucepan and stir in the flour. Gradually add the strained soup and stir until boiling. When at boiling point, whisk in the lobster coral butter. Remove the pan from the heat and stir in the cream. Add salt and pepper to taste. Add the food colouring, if necessary, to obtain a deep orange-pink colour. Add any neat pieces of lobster. Re-heat without boiling the soup.

PRAWN BISQUE

4–6 helpings

100g/4oz butter
250g/8oz cooked shelled prawns
25g/1oz flour
750ml/1½ pints fish stock (page 12) in which prawn shells have been cooked
125ml/¼ pint white wine
125ml/¼ pint court bouillon (page 12)
1 egg yolk
125ml/¼ pint single cream *or* milk *or* half cream and half milk
salt and pepper
lemon juice
a pinch of grated nutmeg

Melt 25g/1oz of the butter in a saucepan. Add the prawns, and toss over gentle heat for 5 minutes. Pound the prawns, gradually working in another 50g/2oz of the butter. Rub the pounded prawn and butter mixture through a sieve, or process briefly in an electric blender. Melt the remaining 25g/1oz butter in a deep saucepan. Stir in the flour and cook gently for 1–2 minutes. Strain the fish stock and gradually stir it into the flour with the wine and court bouillon. Heat to boiling point. Mix the egg yolk with the cream or milk or both. Season the soup and add lemon juice and nutmeg to taste. Whisk the prawn butter into the soup, at just below boiling point, adding a small pat at a time. Add the egg yolk and cream mixture and stir over low heat, without boiling, to thicken the egg.

THE PRAWN.

WHITE FISH CHOWDER

125ml/¼ pint dry white wine
1 litre/2 pints water
bouquet garni
salt and pepper
400g/13oz skinned coley fillets *or*
   other coarse-fleshed white fish

75g/3oz leek
75g/3oz carrot
50g/2oz butter
50g/2oz flour
1 × 5ml spoon/1 teaspoon turmeric
3 × 15ml spoon/3 tablespoons
   chopped parsley

Put the wine, water, bouquet garni, and seasoning in a pan and poach the fish gently in the liquid until tender. Meanwhile, prepare and dice the leek and carrot. Strain the soup into a clean pan. Remove the bouquet garni and cut the fish into 1.25cm/½ inch cubes. Return the pan to the heat and heat to simmering point. Cream the butter and flour to a smooth paste, then add it gradually to the soup, whisking in each addition. Stir in the turmeric. Add the diced vegetables and simmer gently for 7 minutes. Add the fish and the parsley. Simmer for a further 5 minutes.

Serve hot with crusty bread.

White Fish Chowder

HOLLANDAISE SOUP

1 large carrot
10cm/4 inch piece of cucumber
4 × 10ml spoons/4 tablespoons
    small green peas
white stock (page 9) *or* water
25g/1oz butter *or* margarine
4 × 10ml spoons/4 dessertspoons
    flour

1 litre/2 pints white stock (page 9)
2 egg yolks
75ml/3fl oz milk
50ml/2fl oz single cream
salt and pepper
a sprig of tarragon

Cut pea shapes from the carrot and cucumber to give 4 × 10ml spoons/4 dessertspoons of each. Cook the vegetables in a little boiling stock or water until just tender. Put to one side. Melt the fat in a deep saucepan and stir in the flour. Gradually add the 1 litre/2 pints stock, and stir until boiling. Boil for 2–3 minutes, stirring all the time. Remove from the heat and leave to cool slightly. Mix the egg yolks, milk, and cream in a basin. Pour a little hot soup on to the egg yolk mixture, beating well, then whisk the mixture into the rest of the soup. Stir over gentle heat to thicken the yolks, without boiling the soup. Season to taste. Chop the tarragon and add to the soup with the cooked vegetables; add the cooking liquid also, if liked.

Opposite, from the back clockwise:
Lentil and Parsley Soup (page 58),
Garlic Soup (page 61) and
Broad Bean and Ham Soup (page 63)

BROAD BEAN AND HAM SOUP

625g/1¼lb young shelled
    broad beans
125g/5oz ham *or* bacon in 1 piece
4–5 finely chopped sage leaves
2 small onions
1 × 15ml spoon/1 tablespoon
    chopped parsley

1 × 15ml spoon/1 tablespoon
    concentrated tomato purée
750ml/1½ pints water
4–6 slices brown *or* white bread

Cook the broad beans in boiling salted water until tender; then drain. Meanwhile, cut the ham or bacon into very small pieces, about 6mm/¼ inch square. Skin and chop the onions finely. Heat the ham or bacon gently in a saucepan until the fat begins to run. Add the sage, onions, and parsley, and fry quickly for 2–3 minutes to brown the onion a little.

Add the tomato purée and fry gently for a further 2–3 minutes. Add the water, and heat to boiling point. Add the broad beans to the soup, return to simmering point, partly cover the pan, and simmer for 15 minutes. Toast the slices of bread until golden-brown, and place 1 slice in the bottom of each soup bowl. Pour the hot soup over them, and serve quickly.

BROAD BEAN.

VEGETABLE SOUP

4 helpings

500g/1lb vegetables (approx)
15–25g/½–1oz butter, margarine *or* other fat
500ml–1 litre/1–2 pints white stock (page 9) *or* general household stock (page 8)
bouquet garni *or* flavouring herbs
lemon juice

salt and pepper
125ml/¼ pint milk
2 × 10ml spoons/2 dessertspoons thickening (flour, cornflour, ground rice, tapioca, *or* potato) for each 500ml/1 pint puréed soup
cold stock, water *or* milk

FOR CREAM OF VEGETABLE SOUP

add

4–8 × 15ml spoons/4–8 tablespoons single cream and/or
1 egg yolk

Prepare and chop the vegetables. Melt the fat in a deep saucepan, add the vegetables, and fry gently for 5–10 minutes without browning them. Add the stock, bouquet garni or herbs, lemon juice, and seasoning to taste. Heat to boiling point, reduce the heat, and simmer gently until the vegetables are quite soft. Do not overcook.

Remove the bouquet garni. Purée the vegetables and liquid by either rubbing through a fine sieve, or by processing in an electric blender. Add the milk, measure the soup, and return it to a clean pan. Weigh the thickening in the correct proportion and blend it with a little cold stock, water or milk. Stir it into the soup. Bring to the boil, stirring all the time, and cook for 5 minutes. Re-season if required.

Serve with croûtons or Melba toast.

Note To make a cream of vegetable soup, remove the pan from the heat after the soup has been thickened and leave to cool slightly. Add a little of the hot soup to the single cream (which can replace some of the milk in the main recipe) and egg yolk, if using, and beat well. Whisk the mixture into the rest of the soup, Return the soup to gentle heat and re-heat, without boiling, stirring all the time.

SWEETCORN SOUP

4 helpings

3 young sweetcorn cobs *or* 375g/12oz canned sweetcorn kernels (approx)
1 × 10ml spoon/1 dessertspoon butter

500ml/1 pint white stock (page 9)
salt and pepper
a pinch of grated nutmeg

Remove the husks, silks, and tassels from the fresh cobs, and cut off the kernels. Melt the butter in a deep saucepan, add the kernels and scraped cobs, and fry gently for 10 minutes. Add the stock, heat to boiling point, reduce the heat, cover, and simmer gently for 1–1½ hours or until the kernels are quite soft. Remove the scraped cobs and reserve 2 × 15ml spoons/2 tablespoons kernels for the garnish. Rub the rest of the kernels and the liquid through a sieve. Add salt, pepper, and nutmeg to taste. Re-heat the soup to boiling point. Add the reserved kernels.

PIMENTO SOUP

4–6 helpings

3–4 sweet red peppers
1 medium-sized onion
1–2 tomatoes
1 litre/2 pints white stock (page 9)
salt
Cayenne pepper

2 × 10ml spoons/2 dessertspoons cornflour for each 500ml/1 pint puréed soup
cold stock *or* water
sugar

Prepare and slice the vegetables. Put the stock in a deep saucepan and heat to boiling point. Add the vegetables and simmer until soft. Rub the soup through a fine sieve, measure it, and return to the pan. Season to taste. Blend the required amount of cornflour with a little cold stock or water. Stir the cornflour paste into the soup and re-heat until the cornflour has thickened. Add sugar to taste.

MIDSUMMER SOUP

4–6 helpings

5 small carrots
a bunch of radishes
1 small cauliflower
100g/4oz mange-tout peas
1.5 litres/3 pints water
50g/2oz shelled green peas

4 × 15ml spoons/4 tablespoons
 flour
1 × 5ml spoon/1 teaspoon meat
 extract
salt and pepper
1 egg yolk
100ml/4fl oz single cream

Slice the carrots and radishes, break the cauliflower into florets, and top and tail the mange-tout peas. Heat the water to boiling point in a large saucepan. Add all the vegetables and simmer until tender. Blend the flour with a little cold water and stir it into the soup. Simmer gently for another 5 minutes to thicken the soup. Add the meat extract and seasoning to taste. Mix together the yolk and cream. Pour a little hot soup on to the mixture and stir until blended. Add the mixture to the rest of the soup and heat gently, without boiling, to thicken the yolk.

Serve hot with cheese biscuits.

Midsummer Soup

COLD SOUPS

CHILLED PEA SOUP WITH YOGHURT

———— *4 helpings* ————

150g/5oz potatoes
1 medium-sized onion
3–4 lettuce leaves
250g/8oz frozen green peas

500ml/1 pint chicken stock (page 10)
275g/9oz natural yoghurt
salt and pepper
a pinch of sugar

Peel and slice the potatoes and onion, and shred the lettuce leaves. Put with most of the peas into a saucepan with the stock and heat to boiling point. Reduce the heat and simmer for 10 minutes. Rub the soup through a fine sieve, or process in an electric blender. Whisk the yoghurt until the curd is evenly broken down, and add to the soup, reserving 4 × 15ml spoonfuls/4 tablespoons as a garnish. Chill for several hours. Add salt, pepper, and a little sugar to taste. Serve garnished with the remaining peas and yoghurt.

COUNTRY SOUP

———— *6 helpings* ————

625g/1¼lb mixed vegetables (carrot, turnip, onion, leek, celery, tomato)
2 × 15ml spoons/2 tablespoons bacon fat

500ml/1 pint white stock (page 9), water *or* water in which vegetables have been cooked
25g/1oz brown bread
250ml/½ pint milk
salt and pepper

GARNISH

chopped parsley *or* other fresh herbs

Grate the carrot and turnip coarsely, and chop the onion, leek, celery, and tomato. Melt the bacon fat in a deep saucepan, add all the vegetables except the tomato, and fry gently until they begin to brown. Add the stock or water and the tomato. Toast the brown bread, break it up roughly, and add it to the soup. Heat to boiling point, cover, and simmer for 45 minutes or until the vegetables are quite soft. Rub the soup through a fine sieve. Stir in the milk, and season to taste. Re-heat before serving. Garnish each portion with chopped herbs.

Serve with bread croûtons.

THE CUCUMBER.

CUCUMBER AND YOGHURT SOUP

4 helpings

1 small onion
½ cucumber
1 × 15ml spoon/1 tablespoon
  butter
400g/13oz natural yoghurt
250ml/½ pint chicken stock (page
  10)

grated rind and juice of ½ lemon
½ × 15ml spoon/½ tablespoon
  finely chopped mint
salt and pepper

GARNISH

sprigs of mint

Skin and chop the onion finely. Peel the cucumber and cut the flesh into 6mm/¼ inch dice. Melt the butter in a saucepan and cook the onion and cucumber gently, without browning them, for 8–10 minutes. Leave to cool. Whisk the yoghurt until the curd is evenly broken down and add to the soup with the stock. Add the lemon rind and juice, and mint. Season to taste. Chill for several hours. Serve garnished with sprigs of mint.

Country Soup

JELLIED TOMATO SOUP WITH SOURED CREAM

4 helpings

400g/13oz piece honeydew melon (optional)
250ml/½ pint chicken stock (page 10)
2 spring onions
2–3 celery leaves
250ml/½ pint tomato juice
a few drops Worcestershire sauce

3 cloves
a pinch of sugar
a few drops lemon juice
salt
Cayenne pepper
1 × 15ml spoon/1 tablespoon gelatine
2 × 15ml spoons/2 tablespoons water

GARNISH

4 × 10ml spoons/4 dessertspoons soured cream

freshly ground black pepper

Remove the seeds from the melon, if using, and scoop out the flesh with a ball scoop. Chill the melon balls and the chicken stock while preparing the other ingredients.

Chop the onions finely and shred the celery leaves. Put into a large saucepan with the tomato juice, Worcestershire sauce, cloves, sugar, and lemon juice. Season to taste, half cover, and simmer for 10 minute. Remove from the heat and strain into a bowl.

Soften the gelatine in the water in a small heat-proof basin. Stand the basin in a pan of hot water and stir until it has dissolved. Add a little of the strained tomato liquid and stir well. Pour the gelatine into the rest of the tomato liquid and mix well. Add the chilled chicken stock, stir until well blended, and leave to set.

To serve, whisk the jellied soup until frothy. Spoon into 4 chilled bowls, and gently mix in the melon balls, if using. Garnish with soured cream and the black pepper.

CHICKEN AND BEETROOT BROTH

6 helpings

400g/13oz young uncooked beetroots
1 litre/2 pints water
400g/13oz cooked chicken *or* veal
200g/7oz cooked ham
2–3 lettuce hearts
2 long *or* 5 small cucumbers

6 hard-boiled eggs
salt and pepper
a little made English mustard
250ml/½ pint soured cream
1 × 15ml spoon/1 tablespoon chopped fennel leaves *or* stem
6 ice cubes

GARNISH

2 × 15ml spoons/2 tablespoons chopped green part of spring onion *or* chives

Wash and peel the beetroots. Heat the water to boiling point, add the beetroots, cover, and simmer gently for 1 hour. Strain off the liquid and leave to cool. Chop the chicken or veal, the ham, and lettuce hearts into small pieces. Peel and dice the cucumbers. Separate the hard-boiled egg yolks from the whites and sieve the yolks into a bowl. Add salt, pepper, and the mustard to the yolks and gradually stir in the soured cream. Add the chicken, ham, lettuce, and cucumbers, and stir well. Pour the cold beetroot juice over them, and mix well. Chill in a refrigerator for 2–3 hours.

Just before serving, chop the egg white and add it to the soup with the fennel. Put an ice cube in each bowl and pour the soup over it.

Serve with the chopped spring onion tops or chives.

Note The beetroots can be puréed and added to the liquid if liked, to make a very thick soup.

SUMMER SOUP WITH BUTTERMILK

4 helpings

½ green pepper
½ cucumber
250ml/½ pint buttermilk

250ml/½ pint tomato juice
grated rind and juice of ½ lemon
salt and pepper

GARNISH

chopped parsley

Prepare and dice the vegetables. Put the green pepper into a saucepan with a little cold water and heat to boiling point. Drain, and leave to cool. Mix together the buttermilk and tomato juice and add the pepper, cucumber, lemon rind and juice. Season with salt and pepper. Chill for several hours. Serve sprinkled with the chopped parsley.

Summer Soup with Buttermilk

CHILLED AVOCADO SOUP

4 ripe avocado pears
juice of 1 lemon
500ml/1 pint consommé (page 21)
  or canned consommé

250ml/½ pint soured cream
salt and pepper

GARNISH

chopped chives *or* green part of
  spring onions

Scoop out the flesh from the avocado pears, and mix with the lemon juice. Rub through a sieve. Mix the avocado, consommé, and soured cream until blended, and season to taste. Chill in a refrigerator for 2–3 hours. Just before serving, add the chives or spring onions.

THE LEMON.

VEGETABLES

Persons in the flower of youth, having healthy stomachs, and leading active lives, may eat all sorts of vegetables, without inconvenience, save, of course, in excess. The digestive functions possess great energy during the period of youth: the body, to develop itself, needs nourishment. Physical exercise gives an appetite, which it is necessary to satisfy, and vegetables cannot resist the vigorous action of the gastric organs. But for aged persons, the sedentary, or the delicate, it is quite otherwise. Then the gastric power has considerably diminished, the digestive organs have lost their energy, the process of digestion is consequently slower, and the least excess at table is followed by derangement of the stomach for several days. Those who generally digest vegetables with difficulty, should eat them reduced to a pulp or purée, that is to say, with their skins and tough fibres removed. Subjected to this process, vegetables which, when entire, would create flatulence and wind, are then comparatively harmless.

Isabella Beeton 1861

Top: *Stuffed Tomatoes Provençale (page 95)*
Bottom: *Petit Pois à la Française (page 86)*

BROAD BEANS WITH SPANISH SAUCE

1kg/2lb broad beans
1 small onion
375ml/¾ pint beef stock
2–3 sprigs thyme
1 bay leaf
100g/4oz button mushrooms

50g/2oz butter
25g/1oz flour
1 × 5ml spoon/1 teaspoon chopped parsley
1 × 5ml spoon/1 teaspoon lemon juice
salt and pepper

Shell the beans. Skin and chop the onion finely, and put into a saucepan with the stock, thyme, and bay leaf. Bring to the boil, add the beans, and cook for 15–20 minutes, or until tender. Drain and reserve the stock but discard the herbs.

Meanwhile, clean and slice the mushrooms. Melt the butter in a pan and fry the mushrooms; then remove from the pan with a perforated spoon, and add to the beans when cooked. Stir the flour into the remaining butter and cook for 1 minute, stirring all the time. Draw off the heat and gradually stir in the stock from the beans. Return to the heat and bring to the boil, stirring all the time. Add the beans and mushrooms, the parsley and the lemon juice, and season to taste.

BROAD BEAN.

BRETON HARICOT BEANS

200g/7oz haricot beans
1 clove of garlic
1 rasher streaky bacon
2 onions
2 cloves
a bunch of herbs (thyme, sage, savory, marjoram, parsley stalks)

salt and pepper
25g/1oz butter
1 × 15ml spoon/1 tablespoon concentrated tomato purée

GARNISH

1 × 15ml spoon/1 tablespoon chopped parsley

Cover the beans with cold water and leave to soak overnight. Skin and crush the garlic, and chop the bacon. Drain the beans, put into a saucepan, cover with fresh cold water and boil briskly for at least 10 minutes. Skin 1 onion, press the cloves into it, and add to the pan with the garlic, bacon, herbs, and seasoning. Cover and simmer for 1½ hours or until the beans are tender. Drain the beans, reserving 250ml/½ pint of the liquid, and discard the herbs, bacon, and onion. Skin and chop the remaining onion finely. Melt the butter in a pan and fry the onion gently for about 5 minutes. Add the tomato purée and the reserved bean stock. Cover and simmer gently for 10 minutes. Add the drained beans and simmer for a further 10 minutes. Garnish with the chopped parsley before serving.

MRS BEETON'S ASPARAGUS PUDDING

3–4 helpings

150g/5oz asparagus heads
25g/1oz ham
2 × 15ml spoons/2 tablespoons
   flour
salt and pepper

4 eggs
25g/1oz softened butter
milk
fat for greasing

Chop the asparagus heads until they are the size of peas. Mince the ham very finely. Put into a bowl with the flour, asparagus, and seasoning. Beat the eggs well, and add with the butter to the asparagus with enough milk to make the mixture the consistency of a thick batter. Pour into a greased 500ml/1 pint mould or pudding basin. Cover securely with a double layer of buttered greaseproof paper or foil. Steam gently for 2 hours. Turn out on to a warmed serving dish and serve with melted butter poured round, but not over, the pudding.

Mrs Beeton's Asparagus Pudding

BEANS WITH SOURED CREAM

3–4 helpings

400g/13oz runner beans
125ml/¼ pint soured cream
½ × 2.5ml spoon/¼ teaspoon
  grated nutmeg
1 × 2.5ml spoon/½ teaspoon
  caraway seeds

salt and pepper
50g/2oz butter
50g/2oz soft white breadcrumbs

Prepare the beans and boil or steam them until just tender. Drain thoroughly. Mix the soured cream with the nutmeg, caraway seeds, and seasoning. Add the beans and toss well together. Grease a 1 litre/2 pint ovenproof dish with some of the butter and toss the breadcrumbs in it. Sprinkle them on top of the beans. Bake in a moderate oven, 180°C/350°F/Gas 4, for 30 minutes or until the topping is crisp and golden.

POLISH BEETROOT

6 helpings

800g/1lb 10oz cooked beetroot
1 small onion
15g/½ oz butter *or* margarine
2 × 15ml spoons/2 tablespoons
  flour

150g/5oz natural yoghurt
2 × 15ml spoons/2 tablespoons
  finely grated horseradish
salt and pepper
sugar (optional)

GARNISH

1 × 15ml spoon/1 tablespoon
  chopped parsley

Peel and grate the beetroot and skin and finely chop or grate the onion. Melt the fat in a saucepan and fry the onion gently for about 5 minutes. Stir in the flour and cook gently for 1 minute, stirring all the time. Draw off the heat and gradually stir in the yoghurt. Return to the heat, and bring to the boil, stirring all the time, until the sauce thickens. Add the beetroot and horseradish and heat thoroughly. Season to taste, and add sugar to taste, if liked. Serve hot, garnished with the parsley.

BEETROOT.

BOSTON ROAST

6 helpings

300g/10oz haricot beans
1 onion
1 × 15ml spoon/1 tablespoon oil
150g/5oz Cheddar cheese
2 × 15ml spoons/2 tablespoons
   meat *or* vegetable stock *or* water

1 egg
100g/4oz soft white breadcrumbs
salt and pepper
fat for greasing

Cover the beans with cold water and leave to soak overnight. Drain well, put into a saucepan, cover with fresh cold water and boil briskly for at least 10 minutes. Cover and simmer gently for 1½ hours or until the beans are tender. Drain and mash them finely. Skin and chop the onion. Heat the oil in a frying pan and fry the onion until golden-brown. Grate the cheese. Put all the ingredients into a bowl and mix well. Shape the mixture into a loaf, place in a greased baking tin, and cover with buttered greaseproof paper. Bake in a moderate oven, 180°C/350°F/Gas 4, for 45 minutes.

Serve with gravy and vegetables.

Boston Roast

BUTTERED CARROTS

1 helping

500ml/1 pint water
1 chicken stock cube
a pinch of white sugar
3 small carrots
3 spring onions
1 slice of bread

butter
25g/1oz Cheddar cheese
1 × 10ml spoon/1 dessertspoon
    chopped parsley
1 × 10ml spoon/1 dessertspoon
    butter

Bring the water to the boil in a saucepan, crumble in the stock cube and sugar, then draw off the heat. Prepare the carrots, and cut them into slices 6mm/¼ inch thick. Trim the onions, chop the green parts finely and add to the carrots. Halve and add the bulbs. Return the stock to the heat, add the vegetables, and simmer for 10 minutes; then drain. (Reserve the stock for soup or a drink.) Toast the bread, and butter it. Slice the cheese, and place it on the toast. Pile the vegetables on top, sprinkle with the parsley, and dot with the butter. Serve at once.

GERMAN CARROTS

6 helpings

625g/1¼lb carrots
½ small onion
50g/2oz butter *or* margarine
500ml/1 pint stock
extra stock

25g/1oz flour
a good pinch of grated nutmeg
1 × 15ml spoon/1 tablespoon
    chopped parsley
salt and pepper

Prepare the carrots, and skin and chop the onion finely. Melt half the fat in a heavy-based pan. Add the carrots and onion and cook very gently for 10 minutes, shaking the pan frequently so that the vegetables do not stick to the bottom. Pour the stock over the carrots, cover the pan, and simmer gently for 10–15 minutes or until the carrots are tender. Drain the carrots, reserving the cooking liquor, and keep them warm. Make the cooking liquor up to 375ml/¾ pint with extra stock, if necessary. Melt the remaining fat in a saucepan. Add the flour and cook gently for 1 minute, stirring all the time. Draw off the heat and gradually stir in the stock. Return to the heat and bring to the boil, stirring all the time. Add the carrots, nutmeg and parsley, and season to taste. Serve as soon as possible.

CARROTS.

GLAZED CARROTS

6 helpings

625g/1¼lb young carrots
50g/2oz butter
3 sugar lumps

½ × 2.5ml spoon/¼ teaspoon salt
beef stock

GARNISH

1 × 15ml spoon/1 tablespoon
    chopped parsley

Prepare the carrots but leave them whole. Heat the butter in a saucepan. Add the carrots, sugar, salt, and enough stock to half cover the carrots. Cook gently, without a lid, for 15–20 minutes or until the carrots are tender, shaking the pan occasionally. Remove the carrots with a perforated spoon and keep warm. Boil the stock rapidly in the pan until it is reduced to a rich glaze. Replace the carrots, 2–3 at a time, and turn them in the glaze until they are thoroughly coated. Place on a serving dish and garnish with parsley before serving.

Buttered Carrots

CAULIFLOWER CHEESE

———— 4 helpings ————

1 medium-sized firm cauliflower
2 × 15ml spoons/2 tablespoons
   butter *or* margarine
4 × 15ml spoons/4 tablespoons
   flour
200ml/8fl oz milk

125g/5oz grated Cheddar cheese
a pinch of dry mustard
a pinch of Cayenne pepper
salt and pepper
25g/1oz fine dry white
   breadcrumbs

Prepare the cauliflower. Put the head in a saucepan containing enough boiling salted water to half-cover it. Cover the pan, and cook gently for 20–30 minutes until tender. Drain well, reserving 175ml/7fl oz of the cooking water. Break the head carefully into sections, and place in a warmed ovenproof dish. Keep warm under greased greaseproof paper.

Melt the fat in a medium-sized pan, stir in the flour, and cook for 2–3 minutes, stirring all the time, without letting the flour colour. Mix together the milk and reserved cooking water, and gradually add to the pan, stirring all the time to prevent lumps forming. Bring the sauce to the boil, lower the heat, and simmer until thickened. Remove from the heat, and stir in 100g/4oz of the cheese, with the mustard and Cayenne pepper. Season to taste. Stir until the cheese is fully melted, then pour the sauce over the cauliflower. Mix the remaining cheese with the breadcrumbs, and sprinkle them on top. Place in a hot oven, 220°C/425°F/Gas 7, for 7–10 minutes, to brown the top. Serve at once.

Note A mixture of 2 × 15ml spoons/2 tablespoons grated Cheddar cheese and 1 × 15ml spoon/1 tablespoon grated Parmesan cheese can be used for sprinkling, if liked, or 1–2 crumbled, crisply fried rashers of streaky bacon.

CAULIFLOWER WITH RICH MUSHROOM SAUCE

———— 4–6 helpings ————

1kg/2lb cauliflower (approx)
50g/2oz butter
25g/1oz flour
375ml/¾ pint chicken *or* vegetable
   stock *or* milk
100g/4oz button mushrooms
3 egg yolks

1 × 15ml spoon/1 tablespoon
   lemon juice
salt and black pepper
a pinch of grated nutmeg
4–6 slices bread
butter

Prepare the cauliflower. Break it into medium-sized florets and boil or steam them until just tender. Drain thoroughly and keep hot. Melt the 50g/2oz butter in a pan, stir in the flour, and cook for 1 minute. Draw off the heat and gradually stir in the stock or milk. Return to the heat and bring to the boil, stirring all the time, until the sauce thickens. Clean and chop the mushrooms finely, add to the sauce, and simmer gently for 5 minutes. Beat the egg yolks lightly, beat in the lemon juice and 2 × 15ml spoons/2 tablespoons of the hot sauce, then stir into the sauce. Heat gently, but do not allow the sauce to boil after the egg yolks have been added or it will curdle. Season to taste and add the nutmeg.

Toast the bread, cut into rounds, and butter each. Arrange the cauliflower neatly on the rounds, and pour the sauce over. Serve as soon as possible.

Opposite, from the back, clockwise:
Cauliflower Cheese (page 78),
Glazed Carrots (page 77) and
Leeks in Parmesan Sauce (page 80)

STUFFED COURGETTES

1 × 10ml spoon/1 dessertspoon salt	25g/1oz butter for greasing
1 litre/2 pints water	100g/4oz grated Parmesan cheese
1kg/2lb courgettes	chopped herbs

STUFFING

50g/2oz onion	50g/2oz soft white breadcrumbs
1 clove of garlic	1 egg
150g/5oz mushrooms	salt
50ml/2fl oz cooking oil	a pinch of ground mace
150g/5oz lean ham	black pepper

Add the salt to the water in a saucepan and bring it to the boil. Add the courgettes and cook for 8 minutes. Drain and cut in half lengthways. Scoop out the pulp and put it into a small bowl. Keep the skins aside.

To make the stuffing, prepare and chop the onion, garlic, and mushrooms. Heat the oil and sauté the vegetables for 5 minutes. Remove from the heat and keep aside. Mince the ham finely and mix with the breadcrumbs and courgette pulp. Add to the pan, return to the heat and cook for 3 minutes. Turn the mixture into a large bowl. Beat the egg until liquid and season well with salt, mace, and pepper; then add enough egg to the main mixture to make a paste soft enough to be spooned. Season generously.

Fill the courgette skins with the mixture and level the surfaces. Place on a baking tray well greased with soft butter. Sprinkle the stuffed courgettes with the cheese and bake in a moderate oven, 180°C/350°F/Gas 4, for 15–20 minutes until the cheese is melted and golden-brown. Brush once or twice with butter while baking. Sprinkle with chopped herbs, and serve hot.

LEEKS IN PARMESAN SAUCE

1kg/2lb leeks	150ml/6fl oz single cream
1 litre/2 pints water	salt and pepper
1 × 10ml spoon/1 dessertspoon salt	a pinch of grated nutmeg
25g/1oz butter or margarine	1 chicken stock cube
25g/1oz plain flour	50g/2oz grated Parmesan cheese
300ml/12fl oz well-flavoured vegetable stock	

GARNISH

1 × 15ml spoon/1 tablespoon chopped parsley and chives, mixed

Prepare the leeks and keep them whole; tie up in a bundle. Bring the water and salt to the boil in a saucepan and cook the leeks for 20 minutes, then drain well. Put to one side.

Meanwhile, melt the fat in a samll pan, add the flour, and cook for about 4 minutes, stirring until the mixture looks like wet sand. Add the stock gradually, stirring all the time, to make a sauce. Bring to the boil, lower the heat, and stir until the mixture thickens. Stir in the cream, a little salt and simmer gently for 5 minutes. Crumble the stock cube into the sauce. Boil for 5 minutes longer. Remove from the heat, and scatter in half the grated cheese. Untie the bundle of leeks. Put in a long, shallow, flameproof dish and cover with the sauce. Sprinkle with the remaining cheese, and brown under the grill for 5–6 minutes. Sprinkle the herbs on top just before serving.

POLISH CAULIFLOWER

4 helpings

1 large cauliflower
50g/2oz butter *or* margarine
50g/2oz soft white breadcrumbs

2 hard-boiled eggs
1 × 15ml spoon/1 tablespoon
    chopped parsley

Prepare and cook the cauliflower until just tender. Meanwhile, heat the fat in a frying pan and fry the breadcrumbs until they are crisp and golden. Chop the egg whites finely and sieve the yolks. Drain the cauliflower thoroughly and place on a serving dish. Sprinkle the breadcrumbs and then the egg yolk and parsley over the cauliflower. Arrange the chopped egg white round the edge of the dish.

Polish Cauliflower

LETTUCE WITH HERB SAUCE

6 helpings

6 small lettuces
salt
25g/1oz butter *or* margarine
25g/1oz flour
250ml/½ pint chicken *or* vegetable
  stock

1 × 10ml spoon/1 dessertspoon
  chopped chives
1 bay leaf
1 × 10ml spoon/1 dessertspoon
  chopped parsley
pepper

Trim and wash the lettuces. Plunge into boiling salted water for 2 minutes and then drain. Refresh in cold water and drain thoroughly. Melt the fat in a saucepan. Stir in the flour and cook for 1 minute without browning, stirring all the time. Draw off the heat and gradually stir in the stock. Return to the heat and bring to the boil, stirring all the time, until the sauce thickens. Add the herbs and seasoning and then add the lettuces. Cover and cook gently for 30 minutes, stirring from time to time. Remove the bay leaf. Re-season if required before serving.

MUSHROOMS WITH CHEESE

6 helpings

400g/13oz flat mushrooms
butter *or* margarine for greasing
salt and pepper
1 × 15ml spoon/1 tablespoon
  chopped chives
1 × 15ml spoon/1 tablespoon
  chopped parsley

1 × 15ml spoon/1 tablespoon soft
  white breadcrumbs
2 × 15ml spoons/2 tablespoons
  grated Parmesan cheese
25g/1oz butter

Clean the mushrooms and remove the stalks. These can be cooked with the caps or kept and used as a flavouring in another dish. Place the mushrooms, gills uppermost, in a greased ovenproof dish and season. Sprinkle with the chives and parsley. Mix the breadcrumbs and cheese together and sprinkle them over the mushrooms. Melt the butter and sprinkle it over the top. Bake, uncovered, in a fairly hot oven, 190°C/375°F/Gas 5, for 25 minutes.

MUSHROOMS.

SPICED LENTILS

500g/1lb red lentils
1 litre/2 pints water
1 × 2.5ml spoon/½ teaspoon sea
  salt *or* 1 × 5ml spoon/1 teaspoon
  table salt
1 onion
1 × 5ml spoon/1 teaspoon turmeric
1 × 5ml spoon/1 teaspoon crushed
  root *or* ground ginger

3 tomatoes
2 whole cardamoms
3 × 15ml spoons/3 tablespoons
  cooking oil
1 × 5ml spoon/1 teaspoon crushed
  garlic
1 × 5ml spoon/1 teaspoon ground
  coriander
a pinch of chilli powder

GARNISH

chopped fresh coriander leaves   finely chopped *or* grated onion

Put the lentils into a large pan and cover with the water and salt. Bring to the boil, reduce the heat, and simmer for 30–45 minutes until tender. Drain and put to one side.

Meanwhile, skin and chop the onion, and mix with the turmeric and ginger. Chop the tomatoes, and crush the cardamoms in a pestle and mortar, or grind in a coffee or nut mill. Heat the oil in a large deep frying pan, add the onion, ginger and turmeric, and fry gently until soft and lightly browned. Add the tomatoes and all the remaining ingredients, and fry for 3–4 minutes, stirring all the time. Remove from the heat.

Add the lentils to the mixture in the pan, and mix thoroughly to coat them with oil. Replace over moderate heat, and cook until well heated through and quite mushy. Serve very hot, sprinkled with the coriander leaves and onion.

Note Although hot and spicy, this dish is not as hot as a curry. It can be served as an accompaniment to any pasta, pulse or plainly cooked root vegetable dish, or with a green vegetable salad as a main course dish.

Spiced Lentils

STUFFED MUSHROOMS

6 helpings

12 large flat mushrooms
fat for greasing
1 medium-sized onion
25g/1oz butter *or* margarine
50g/2oz cooked ham
1 × 15ml spoon/1 tablespoon soft
    white breadcrumbs

1 × 10ml spoon/1 dessertspoon
    grated Parmesan cheese
1 × 10ml spoon/1 dessertspoon
    chopped parsley
white wine
salt and pepper

Clean the mushrooms and remove the stalks. Place the caps in a well-greased ovenproof dish, gills uppermost, and chop the stalks finely. Skin and chop the onion finely. Melt the fat in a pan and fry the mushroom stalks and onion gently for 5 minutes. Chop the ham finely and add to the onion mixture together with the breadcrumbs, cheese, and parsley. Add enough white wine just to bind the mixture together, and season well. Divide the stuffing mixture between the mushroom caps. Cover and bake in a fairly hot oven, 190°C/375°F/Gas 5, for 25 minutes.

Note If liked, the mushrooms can be served on croûtes of toast or fried bread.

ONION.

ONIONS AND APPLES

4 helpings

300g/10oz onions
400g/13oz cooking apples
3 × 15ml spoons/3 tablespoons
    butter *or* margarine

1 × 10ml spoon/1 dessertspoon
    sugar
salt and pepper

Skin and blanch the onions. Drain and cut them into rings. Peel, core, and slice the apples. Melt the fat in a pan and add the onions, apples and sugar. Cover and simmer gently for about 30 minutes or until tender. Season to taste and serve.

ONIONS IN CIDER WITH TOMATOES

6 helpings

6 large onions
200g/7oz tomatoes
50g/2oz butter *or* margarine
2 bay leaves
2 cloves

2 × 15ml spoons/2 tablespoons
    cider
250ml/½ pint vegetable stock
salt and pepper

Skin and blanch the onions. Drain and cut them into rings. Skin and slice the tomatoes. Melt the fat in a pan. Add the onion rings and fry gently until golden. Add the tomatoes, bay leaves, cloves, cider, and stock. Cover and simmer gently for 45 minutes. Season to taste and serve with the cooking liquor.

GLAZED ONIONS

4 helpings

400g/13oz button onions
chicken stock
salt and pepper
1 × 15ml spoon/1 tablespoon light
   soft brown sugar

25g/1oz butter
a pinch of grated nutmeg

Skin the onions and put them in a saucepan into which they just fit in one layer. Add just enough stock to cover them. Heat to simmering point, and simmer for 15–20 minutes until the onions are just tender, adding a very little extra hot stock if needed. When the onions are ready, the stock should be reduced almost to a glaze. Remove from the heat, and add the rest of the ingredients. Turn the onions over with a spoon to blend the extra seasonings well with the stock and to coat the onions. Return to the heat, and shake the onions in the pan, until the glaze and fat give them a shiny brown coating. Serve at once, with the remaining syrupy glaze.

Note Glazed onions are often used as a garnish.

Stuffed Mushrooms

PARSNIP AND APPLE CASSEROLE

6 helpings

400g/13oz parsnips
200ml/8fl oz apple sauce
fat for greasing
75g/3oz brown sugar
salt
1 × 2.5ml spoon/½ teaspoon
  grated nutmeg

1 × 15ml spoon/1 tablespoon
  lemon juice
75g/3oz butter
75g/3oz soft white breadcrumbs
½ × 2.5ml spoon/¼ teaspoon
  paprika

Prepare and boil or steam the parsnips. Mash or sieve them. Arrange with the apple sauce in layers in a greased casserole. Sprinkle each layer with brown sugar, salt, nutmeg, lemon juice, and flakes of butter. Top with the breadcrumbs and sprinkle with paprika. Cook in a fairly hot oven, 190°C/375°F/Gas 5, for 30 minutes.

PETITS POIS À LA FRANÇAISE

6 helpings

1 lettuce heart
1 bunch spring onions
50g/2oz butter
750g/1½ lb fresh shelled *or* frozen
  peas

salt and pepper
a pinch of sugar

Shred the lettuce and chop the spring onions. Melt the butter in a pan, add the lettuce, spring onions, peas, seasoning, and sugar. Cover and simmer gently for 10–15 minutes or until the peas are very tender. Re-season if required before serving.

Note Frozen peas may take even less than 10 minutes; well-grown fresh garden peas may take 20–25 minutes.

GREEN PEA.

SCALLOPED OKRA AND TOMATOES

300g/10oz okra
milk
200g/7oz tomatoes
salt and pepper
3 × 15ml spoons/3 tablespoons
   butter *or* margarine

25g/1oz flour
2 × 15ml spoons/2 tablespoons soft
   white breadcrumbs

Wash the okra and cook in boiling salted water for 15 minutes. Drain, reserving the cooking liquor. Make the liquor up to 250ml/½ pint with milk, if necessary. Cut the okra into small pieces and slice the tomatoes. Divide the okra and tomatoes between 6 scallop shells or small ramekin dishes. Season with salt and pepper. Melt 2 × 15ml spoons/2 tablespoons of the fat in a pan. Stir in the flour and cook for 1 minute without browning, stirring all the time. Draw off the heat and gradually stir in the cooking liquor and milk. Return to the heat and bring to the boil, stirring all the time, until the sauce thickens. Re-season if required. Pour this over the okra and tomatoes. Sprinkle with the breadcrumbs and dot with the remaining fat. Bake in a fairly hot oven, 190°C/375°F/Gas 5, for 15–20 minutes. Serve hot in the scallop shells or ramekin dishes.

Scalloped Okra and Tomatoes

PEPPERS WITH APPLE

3–4 helpings

1 large cooking apple
100g/4oz Gruyère cheese
3–4 large green peppers
1 small green pepper
25g/1oz butter *or* margarine

25g/1oz flour
250ml/½ pint milk
salt and freshly ground black
  pepper
butter *or* margarine for greasing

GARNISH (OPTIONAL)

1 thickly sliced tomato

3–4 button mushroom caps

Peel, core, and chop the apple into small pieces. Grate the cheese. Wash the large peppers and cut off the tops. Discard the membranes and the seeds, but keep the caps. Blanch the peppers and their caps. Drain. Chop the small pepper finely. Melt the fat, stir in the flour, and cook together over gentle heat for 2–3 minutes, stirring all the time. Do not let the flour colour. Draw off the heat and gradually stir in the milk, without letting lumps form. Return to the heat, bring to the boil, and simmer until very thick, stirring occasionally. Season to taste. Mix in the chopped apple, grated cheese, and chopped pepper. Trim the bases of the other peppers so that they stand steadily, cut sides uppermost. Spoon the stuffing mixture into the peppers and replace the caps. Place the peppers, cut side uppermost on a lightly greased baking tray. Bake in a cool oven, 150°C/300°F/Gas 2, for 25–30 minutes. Garnish, if liked, with the sliced tomato and mushroom caps before serving.

POTATOES BYRON

4–6 helpings

1kg/2lb potatoes
salt and pepper
a good pinch of grated nutmeg
100g/4oz butter

flour
125ml/¼ pint single cream
50g/2oz grated Parmesan cheese

Wash and bake the potatoes in their skins in a fairly hot oven, 190–200°C/375–400°F/Gas 5–6, for 1–1½ hours. When cooked, cut them in half and scoop the pulp into a basin. Season with salt, pepper, and nutmeg. Add 75g/3oz of the butter and beat the mixture well with a wooden spoon. Divide into 6 or 8 portions and mould into medallion shapes, 1.25–2.5cm/½–1 inch thick, on a floured surface. Heat the remaining butter in a frying pan and fry the potatoes gently on both sides until golden-brown. Remove from the pan and put in an ovenproof dish. Either spoon the cream over each potato medallion and sprinkle with the cheese, or add half the cheese to the white sauce, spoon it over the potatoes, then sprinkle with the remaining cheese. Place the dish under a moderate grill until the cheese is golden-brown.

PEASE PUDDING

6 helpings

625g/1¼lb split peas
1 small onion
bouquet garni

salt and pepper
50g/2oz butter *or* margarine
2 eggs

Soak the peas overnight. Drain, put into a pan, and cover with fresh cold water. Skin the onion and add to the pan with the bouquet garni and seasoning. Cover and simmer the peas slowly for about 2–2½ hours or until they are tender. Drain thoroughly and sieve or process in an electric blender. Cut the fat into small pieces, beat the eggs until liquid, and add both to the pea purée with the seasoning. Beat well together. Place the mixture in a floured cloth and tie tightly. Simmer gently in boiling salted water for 1 hour. Remove from the pan, take out of the cloth, and serve very hot.

Serve with sausages or pickled pork.

Pease Pudding

TORTILLA ESPAGNOLA

(Spanish Omelet)

———— 4 helpings ————

750g/1½lb potatoes   salt
250g/8oz onions   6 eggs
olive oil for shallow frying

Peel and dice the potatoes. Skin and slice the onions, and mix them together. Put enough oil into a large frying pan to cover the bottom by 6mm/¼ inch. Heat the oil until very hot, then add the potatoes and onions, and sprinkle with salt. Fry gently for about 20 minutes until soft but not crisp. Turn over or stir gently from time to time. Remove the vegetables from the pan with a perforated spoon.

Beat the eggs lightly with a pinch of salt, and stir into the fried vegetable mixture. Drain off any oil, clean the pan, and heat 1 × 5ml spoon/1 teaspoon oil in it until very hot. Pour in the egg and vegetable mixture, and cook briefly, shaking the pan vigorously to prevent the mixture sticking. Slide the half-cooked omelet on to a large plate, turn it over on to a second plate, then slide it back into the pan, uncooked side down. Cook for another 2–3 minutes to brown the second side, shaking as before.

The finished tortilla should be about 2.5cm/1 inch thick, crisp on the outside, and juicy in the middle.

Serve with a green salad.

DUCHESSE POTATOES

———— Makes 500g/1lb (approx) ————

500g/1lb old potatoes   a little grated nutmeg (optional)
25g/1oz butter or margarine   butter or margarine for greasing
1 egg or 2 egg yolks   a little beaten egg for brushing
salt and pepper

Prepare the potatoes, and boil or steam them. Drain thoroughly, and sieve. Beat in the fat and egg or egg yolks. Season to taste with salt and pepper and add the nutmeg, if used. Spoon the mixture into a piping bag fitted with a large rose nozzle and pipe rounds of potato on to a greased baking tray. Brush with a little beaten egg. Bake in a fairly hot oven, 200°C/400°F/Gas 6, for about 15 minutes or until the potatoes are a good golden-brown.

Note The potatoes can be piped on to the baking tray and then baked when required. If a piping bag is not available, shape the potato into diamonds, rounds or triangles. Criss-cross the tops with a knife, brush with the egg, and bake as above.

POTATOES PARISIENNE

4–6 helpings

1kg/2lb potatoes
25g/1oz butter
1 × 15ml spoon/1 tablespoon oil
½ × 2.5ml spoon/¼ teaspoon salt
3 × 15ml spoons/3 tablespoons
    softened butter

3 × 15ml spoons/3 tablespoons
    chopped fresh mixed herbs
    (parsley, chives, tarragon)
pepper

Peel the potatoes and cut into small, round balls, using a potato ball scoop. Dry in a clean cloth. Heat the butter and oil in a frying pan large enough to hold all the potatoes in 1 layer. Put in the potatoes and coat evenly in the fat. Fry them gently until the potatoes are a light golden colour all over. Reduce the heat, sprinkle with the salt and cover the pan. Continue frying very gently for 12–15 minutes, shaking the pan frequently, until the potatoes are tender. Drain off the fat. Raise the heat and shake the potatoes in the pan until sizzling. Remove from the heat, add the softened butter and herbs, season well with pepper, and roll the potatoes round the pan until coated with herbs. Arrange round a meat dish or serve separately in a warmed dish.

Note Carrots, turnips, and similar vegetables can be cooked in the same way as the potatoes.

Tortilla Espagnola

POTATOES LYONNAISE

6 helpings

1kg/2lb potatoes
250g/8oz onions
75g/3oz butter *or* margarine

salt and pepper
1 × 15ml spoon/1 tablespoon
  chopped parsley

Scrub the potatoes, but do not peel them. Boil or steam them in their skins until tender. Drain, peel, and cut into slices 6mm /¼ inch thick. Skin and slice the onions thinly. Melt the fat in a frying pan and fry the onions gently until they are just golden. Remove from the pan, put on one side, and keep warm. Add the potatoes to the pan and fry on both sides until crisp and golden. Replace the onions in the pan and mix with the potatoes. Season to taste with salt and pepper, turn into a serving dish, and sprinkle with the parsley.

POTATOES.

POTATO CROQUETTES

Makes 12–15

500g/1lb old potatoes
25g/1oz butter *or* margarine
1 egg *or* 2 egg yolks
salt and pepper
1 × 5ml spoon/1 teaspoon chopped
  parsley *or* 2 × 15ml spoons/2
  tablespoons grated Parmesan *or*
  Cheddar cheese (optional)

2 eggs
flour for dusting
dried white breadcrumbs for
  coating
fat *or* oil for deep frying

Prepare the potatoes and boil or steam them. Drain thoroughly, and sieve. Beat in the fat and egg or egg yolks, and season to taste. Add the parsley or grated cheese, if used. Beat the eggs until liquid, form the potato into balls or cylindrical rolls, dust with flour, and coat twice with egg and breadcrumbs. If possible, chill for 1 hour before frying. Heat the fat or oil to 190°C/375°F, and fry the potato croquettes or balls until golden-brown. Drain thoroughly and serve as soon as possible.

Opposite from the left:
Potatoes Lyonnaise (page 92),
Potatoes Byron (page 88) and
Potatoes Parisienne (page 91)

ITALIAN SPINACH

4 helpings

25g/1oz butter *or* margarine
1kg/2lb spinach
salt and pepper
25g/1oz sultanas

1 clove of garlic
2 × 15ml spoons/2 tablespoons
  olive oil
25g/1oz pine kernels

Melt the butter in a pan, add the wet spinach leaves, season with salt, then cover and cook slowly for about 10 minutes or until the spinach is tender. Drain thoroughly; then chop coarsely. Cover the sultanas with boiling water for 1 minute to plump them; then drain thoroughly. Skin and crush the garlic. Heat the oil in a wide pan. Add the spinach, garlic, and seasoning. Turn the spinach over and over in the pan to heat it thoroughly without frying. Add the sultanas and nuts and serve hot.

CORN PUDDING

6 helpings

100g/4oz plain flour
1 × 5ml spoon/1 teaspoon salt
1 × 2.5ml spoon/½ teaspoon black
  pepper
2 eggs

500ml/1 pint milk
400g/13oz fresh *or* frozen
  sweetcorn kernels
fat for greasing

Sift the flour, salt, and pepper. Beat the eggs until liquid and add them to the flour, stirring well. Beat together with the milk and then the corn to form a batter. Turn into a greased 1.5 litre/3 pint pie or ovenproof dish and bake in a moderate oven, 180°C/350°F/Gas 4, for 1 hour. Serve hot.

STUFFED TOMATOES PROVENÇALE

4 helpings

8 medium-sized tomatoes
salt and pepper
50g/2oz onions *or* shallots
1 small clove of garlic
1 × 15ml spoon/1 tablespoon olive
  oil

25g/1oz butter
75–100g/3–4oz soft white
  breadcrumbs
1 × 15ml spoon/1 tablespoon
  chopped parsley

Halve the tomatoes crossways. Remove the pips and juice and place the tomatoes in an ovenproof dish. Season lightly with salt and pepper. Skin and chop the onion or shallots finely. Skin and crush the garlic. Heat the oil in a pan and fry the onion and garlic gently without browning. Add the butter and heat until melted; then add the breadcrumbs and parsley. Season to taste and mix well together. Spoon this mixture into the tomato halves. Bake in a hot oven, 220°C/425°F/Gas 7, for 15 minutes or until the breadcrumbs are lightly browned.

THE TOMATO.

TOMATO AND ONION PIE

4 helpings

400g/13oz onions, preferably
   Spanish
50g/2oz butter
800g/1lb 10oz tomatoes

50g/2oz Cheddar cheese
fat for greasing
salt and pepper
50g/2oz soft white breadcrumbs

Skin the onions, put into a bowl, and cover with boiling water. Leave for 5 minutes, drain, dry thoroughly, and cut into slices. Melt half the butter in a pan and fry the onions until golden-brown. Skin and slice the tomatoes, and grate the cheese. Place the onions and tomatoes in alternate layers in a greased pie dish, sprinkle each layer lightly with salt and pepper and liberally with cheese and some of the breadcrumbs. Cover the whole with a layer of breadcrumbs and dot with the remaining butter. Bake in a fairly hot oven, 190°C/375°F/Gas 5, for 45 minutes.

Italian Spinach and *Corn Pudding*

VEGETABLE AND NUT FRICASSÉE

1 medium-sized onion
2 sticks celery
25g/1oz margarine
50g/2oz flour
500ml/1 pint milk

75g/3oz cashew nuts *or* pine
  kernels
salt and pepper
2–3 × 15ml spoons/2–3
  tablespoons single cream

GARNISH

cooked spinach *or* green peas   cooked carrots

Skin the onion, and chop finely with the celery. Melt the margarine in a pan and fry the onion and celery gently for a few minutes, without browning. Stir in the flour and cook for 1 minute. Draw off the heat and gradually stir in the milk. Return to the heat and bring to the boil, stirring all the time, until the sauce thickens. Add the nuts and seasoning. Cover the pan, reduce the heat, and simmer gently for 15 minutes. Stir in the cream and re-season if required.

Make a border of the spinach or peas on a hot dish. Pour the fricassée into the centre of the dish and garnish with the carrot, cut into matchsticks. Serve hot.

RATATOUILLE

250g/8oz onions (approx)
1 clove of garlic
100g/4oz green pepper (approx)
200g/7oz aubergine (approx)
200g/7oz courgettes
400g/13oz tomatoes

4 × 15ml spoons/4 tablespoons
  olive oil
sat and pepper
1 × 2.5ml spoon/½ teaspoon
  coriander seeds

GARNISH

1 × 15ml spoon/1 tablespoon
  chopped parsley

Skin the onions and slice in rings. Skin and crush the garlic. Remove the membranes and seeds from the pepper and cut the flesh into thin strips. Cut the unpeeled aubergine and courgettes into 1.25cm/½ inch slices. Skin and chop the tomatoes roughly.

Heat 2 × 15ml spoons/2 tablespoons of the oil in a pan and gently fry the onions, garlic, and pepper for about 10 minutes. Add the remaining oil, the aubergine, and the courgettes. Cover and simmer gently for 30 minutes, stirring occasionally to prevent the vegetables from sticking to the bottom. Add the tomatoes, seasoning and coriander seeds, and simmer for a further 15 minutes. Serve hot or cold, garnished with the parsley.

GARLIC.

MARROW WITH TOMATOES

4–6 helpings

400g/13oz tomatoes
25g/1oz butter *or* margarine

1 medium-sized marrow
salt and pepper

GARNISH

1 × 10ml spoon/1 dessertspoon
  chopped parsley

1 × 10ml spoon/1 dessertspoon
  chopped chives

Skin the tomatoes and cut into slices. Melt the fat in a saucepan. Add the tomatoes and cook gently for 10 minutes. Peel the marrow, discard the seeds, and cut the flesh into 2.5cm/1 inch squares. Add to the tomatoes and season with salt and pepper. Cover the pan with a tight-fitting lid and cook the marrow gently for 20 minutes or until tender. Re-season if required before serving. Garnish with the parsley and chives.

Marrow with Tomatoes

PEPERONATA

4 helpings

300g/10oz tomatoes
1 large onion
1 large red pepper
2 large green peppers
1 large yellow pepper *or* 1 extra red
   pepper

3 × 15ml spoons/3 tablespoons
   olive oil
1 × 2.5ml spoon/½ teaspoon
   coriander seeds (optional)
salt and pepper

Skin the tomatoes, cut into quarters, and remove the seeds. Skin and slice the onion. Skin the peppers, remove the membranes and seeds, and chop the flesh. Heat the oil in a frying pan, add the onion, and fry for 5 minutes. Lightly crush the coriander seeds, if used. Add the tomatoes, peppers, coriander seeds, and seasoning to the pan. Cover and cook gently for 1 hour, stirring from time to time. Re-season if required before serving. Serve hot or cold.

VEGETABLE CASSEROLE

4–6 helpings

400g/13oz onions
2 cloves garlic
2 green peppers
400g/13oz courgettes
2 medium-sized aubergines
400g/13oz tomatoes
2 × 15ml spoons/2 tablespoons oil
200g/7oz mushrooms
75g/3oz concentrated tomato purée
2 bay leaves

1 × 15ml spoon/1 tablespoon
   chopped parsley
1 × 5ml spoon/1 teaspoon chopped
   marjoram
1 × 5ml spoon/1 teaspoon chopped
   thyme
salt and pepper
250ml/½ pint vegetable stock *or*
   water
400g/13oz potatoes
25g/1oz butter

Skin and chop the onions and skin and crush the garlic. Remove the membranes and seeds from the peppers and chop the flesh. Slice the unpeeled courgettes and aubergines and skin and slice the tomatoes. Heat the oil in a frying pan and fry the onions, garlic, and peppers for 5 minutes. Turn into a 3 litre/6 pint casserole with the courgettes, aubergines, tomatoes, mushrooms, tomato purée, herbs, and seasoning. Mix well and pour in the stock or water. Peel and slice the potatoes thinly, and arrange on the top. Dot with the butter, and cover. Bake in a moderate oven, 180°C/350°F/Gas 4, for 1 hour. Remove the lid and bake for a further 30 minutes or until the potatoes are golden-brown.

MIXED VEGETABLES

6 helpings

750g/1½lb mixed vegetables
  parsnips, turnips, carrots, leeks,
  cauliflower *or* broad beans, peas,
  spring onions, tomatoes, new
  carrots, new turnips

25g/1oz butter *or* margarine
100–150ml/4–6fl oz boiling water
salt and pepper

GARNISH

1 × 15ml spoon/1 tablespoon
  chopped parsley

Prepare the vegetables; then thinly slice the parsnips, turnips,
carrots, and leeks, if used, splitting the slices into halves or
quarters if large. Break the cauliflower into florets. Leave most of
the other vegetables whole, cutting the larger carrots into thick
slices, trimming the spring onions rather short, and cutting the
tomatoes into wedges. Melt the fat in a heavy-based saucepan.
Add the vegetables at intervals, starting with those which take the
longest time to cook. Put the lid on the pan after each addition and
toss the vegetables in the fat. (Do not add the tomatoes until 5
minutes before serving.) Add the boiling water and salt; use very
little water with the beans and new carrots, etc. Simmer gently
until the vegetables are tender. Season with pepper and serve hot,
garnished with the parsley.

Peperonata

NUT MINCE

6 helpings

200g/7oz shelled nuts
1 medium-sized onion
25g/1oz margarine
150g/5oz dried breadcrumbs
1 × 15ml spoon/1 tablespoon
   mushroom ketchup *or* any
   similar sauce

375ml/¾ pint (approx) vegetable
   stock
salt and pepper

Pass the nuts through a nut mill, process them in an electric blender, or chop very finely. Skin and grate the onion. Melt the margarine in a frying pan and fry the nuts, onion, and breadcrumbs until pale golden. Stir in the ketchup and stock, adding a little extra stock if the mixture is too dry. Season to taste and simmer gently for 20–30 minutes. Serve hot.

THE WALNUT.

POULTRY

A noble dish is a turkey, roast or boiled.
A Christmas dinner, with the middle
classes of this empire, would scarcely be
a Christmas dinner without its turkey;
and we can hardly imagine an object of
greater envy than is presented by a
respected portly paterfamilias carving, at
the season devoted to good cheer and
genial charity, his own fat turkey, and
carving it well.

Isabella Beeton 1861

Left: *Duckling in Red Wine (page 125)*
Below: *Braised Turkey (page 123)*

CHICKEN

ROAST CHICKEN WITH HONEY AND ALMONDS

4–6 helpings

1 roasting chicken
½ lemon
salt and pepper
3 × 15ml spoons/3 tablespoons
  honey

50g/2oz blanched almonds
a pinch of powdered saffron
  (optional)
2 × 15ml spoons/2 tablespoons oil

Truss the chicken. Rub all over with the cut lemon, then sprinkle with salt and pepper. Line a roasting tin with a piece of foil large enough to cover the bird and to meet over the top. Put the bird on the foil, and rub it all over with honey. Slice the almonds and sprinkle them and the saffron, if used, over the bird. Pour the oil over the bird very gently. Wrap it completely in the foil, keeping it clear of the skin. Seal by folding over the edges. Roast in a moderate–fairly hot oven, 180–190°C/350–375°F/Gas 4–5, for about 1½ hours, until tender. Unwrap the foil for the last 10 minutes to allow the breast to brown.

Roast Chicken with Honey and Almonds

QUICK CURRIED CHICKEN OR FOWL

(Country Captain)

4–6 helpings

1 cooked chicken *or* fowl
2 large onions
50g/2oz chicken fat *or* butter
1 × 15ml spoon/ 1 tablespoon curry
  powder
1 × 10ml spoon/1 dessertspoon
  curry paste
1 × 15ml spoon/1 tablespoon flour
375ml/¾ pint stock

1 large sweet apple
1 × 10ml spoon/1 dessertspoon
  chutney
1 × 15ml spoon/1 tablespoon
  lemon juice
salt and pepper
50g/2oz whole blanched almonds
fat for frying

GARNISH

lemon butterflies

Cut the bird into neat pieces. Keep any bones and trimmings for stock. Skin and chop the onions. Heat the chicken fat or butter, and fry the onions slowly until lightly browned. Add the curry powder, paste, and flour, and fry gently for 3 minutes. Stir in the stock gradually and bring to the boil. Peel, core, and dice the apple, and add to the mixture, together with the chutney, lemon juice, and seasoning. Simmer gently for 30 minutes, stirring occasionally. Add the chicken pieces and heat through slowly. Re-season if required.

Fry the almonds for a few minutes until golden-brown. Serve the chicken curry on a hot dish with the almonds sprinkled on top. Garnish with lemon butterflies.

Plain boiled rice and chutney should be served separately as accompaniments.

Quick Curried Chicken

HOT CHICKEN LIVER MOUSSE

4 helpings

1 × 15ml spoon/1 tablespoon
    butter *or* margarine
2 × 15ml spoons/2 tablespoons
    plain flour
150ml/¼ pint milk
salt and pepper
225g/8oz chicken livers

1 egg
1 egg yolk
3 × 15ml spoons/3 tablespoons
    double cream
1 × 15ml spoon/1 tablespoon dry
    sherry
butter for greasing

GARNISH

chopped chives

Put the butter or margarine in a medium-sized saucepan with the flour and milk. Whisking all the time over a moderate heat, bring to the boil and cook for 2–3 minutes until thickened and smooth. Season to taste. Leave the sauce to become cold, stirring from time to time.

Remove the skin and tubes from the livers. Either process in an electric blender, or mince twice to obtain a purée. Beat in the egg and egg yolk. Add the sauce, cream and sherry. Pour into 4 well-buttered 150ml/¼ pint cocotte dishes. Place in a baking tin, and fill it with enough boiling water to come half-way up the sides of the dishes. Cook in a moderate oven, 180°C/350°C/Gas 4, for 25–30 minutes until a fine skewer inserted in the centre comes out clean. Allow to stand for a few minutes before turning out. Sprinkle with chives and serve hot.

BUTTER-DISH.

STUFFED CHICKEN LEGS

4 helpings

4 cooked drumsticks
salt and Cayenne pepper
1 × 15ml spoon/1 tablespoon
    vegetable oil
2 × 15ml spoons/2 tablespoons
    white breadcrumbs
1 × 2.5ml spoon/½ teaspoon
    mixed herbs

1 × 5ml spoon/1 teaspoon chopped
    parsley
1 small onion
1 × 2.5ml spoon/½ teaspoon
    grated lemon rind
1 egg
4 gammon rashers
fat for greasing

GARNISH

parsley sprigs

Season each drumstick with salt and Cayenne pepper and moisten with oil. Mix the breadcrumbs, herbs, and finely chopped parsley in a basin. Skin, blanch, and chop the onion finely and add it to the basin together with the lemon rind. Moisten the mixture with the egg. Spread each gammon rasher with this stuffing, and wrap one rasher around each drumstick. Tie or skewer the rasher securely in place. Put the drumsticks on a greased baking tray and cook in a moderate oven, 180°C/350°F/Gas 4, for 20 minutes; then cover them with foil, and cook for a further 20 minutes. Garnish with parsley sprigs.

Serve at once on trimmed slices of hot buttered toast.

CHICKEN KIEV

4 helpings

4 chicken breast and wing joints	1 egg
salt and pepper	100g/4oz soft white breadcrumbs
flour for coating	(approx)
	fat *or* oil for deep frying

BUTTER FILLING

finely grated rind of ½ lemon	salt and freshly ground black
1 × 15ml spoon/1 tablespoon	pepper
chopped parsley	2 small cloves garlic
100g/4oz softened butter	

GARNISH

lemon wedges	parsley sprigs

Make the butter filling first. Work the lemon rind and parsley thoroughly into the butter, and season to taste. Crush and work in the garlic. Form the butter into a roll, wrap in clingfilm and chill.

To prepare the chicken, cut off the wing pinions. Turn the joints, flesh side up, and cut out all bones except the wing bone which is left in place. Do not cut right through the flesh. Flatten out the boned meat, cover with greaseproof paper, and beat lightly with a cutlet bat or heavy knife. Cut the seasoned butter into 4 long pieces and place one on each piece of chicken. Fold the flesh over the butter to enclose it completely, and secure with wooden cocktail sticks. The wing bone should protrude at one end of each cutlet. Season the flour with salt and pepper and roll each piece of chicken in it. Beat the egg lightly on a plate. Roll or dip the chicken in the egg, coating each cutlet completely; then roll each in the breadcrumbs. Heat the fat or oil to 160–165°C/320–329°F, and deep fry 2 cutlets at a time until they are golden-brown and cooked through. Drain thoroughly and keep hot while frying the remaining two. Place the cutlets on a warmed serving dish with the bones overlapping in the centre. Remove the cocktail sticks and garnish with lemon wedges and parsley before serving.

FRITOT OF CHICKEN

4–6 helpings

1 cold cooked chicken	fat *or* oil for deep frying

MARINADE

a slice of onion	1 × 2.5ml spoon/½ teaspoon dried
a sprig of parsley	mixed herbs
2 × 15ml spoons/2 tablespoons	salt and pepper
olive oil	
1 × 15ml spoon/1 tablespoon	
lemon juice	

BATTER

100g/4oz flour	1 × 15ml spoon/1 tablespoon
125ml/¼ pint tepid water	vegetable oil
a pinch of salt	2 egg whites

GARNISH

parsley sprigs

Cut the chicken into joints. Remove the skin and any excess fat, and place the joints in a deep bowl.

Make the marinade. Chop the onion finely with the parsley, and mix together with the other marinade ingredients. Pour it over the chicken joints and allow to stand for 1½ hours, turning them occasionally.

Make the batter by mixing the flour, water, salt, and oil together until smooth. Beat well, and allow to stand for 1 hour. Then whisk the egg whites until stiff, and fold into the batter.

Drain the chicken joints, dry well with soft kitchen paper, and dip each piece in the batter. Fry the joints in hot fat or oil until golden on all sides. Drain on soft kitchen paper.

Garnish with parsley, and serve with Tartare sauce.

CHICKEN CHASSEUR

4–6 helpings

1 roasting chicken
salt and pepper
25g/1 oz flour
1 × 15ml spoon/1 tablespoon
  cooking oil
50g/2oz butter
3 tomatoes *or* 1 × 15ml spoon/1
  tablespoon concentrated tomato
  purée

25g/1oz onion *or* shallot
175g/6oz button mushrooms
150ml/6fl oz dry white wine
275ml/11fl oz chicken stock
1 sprig each of fresh tarragon,
  chervil, and parsley

Divide the chicken into 8 serving portions. Season the flour with salt and pepper, and use to dust the portions. Heat the oil and butter in a frying pan, and fry the chicken pieces until tender and browned all over, allowing 15–20 minutes for dark meat (drumsticks and thighs), 10–20 minutes for light meat (breast and wings). When tender, remove from the pan, drain on soft kitchen paper, and transfer to a warmed serving dish. Cover loosely with buttered paper and keep hot.

Skin and chop the tomatoes if used, and the onion or shallot. Put the onion or shallot into the pan, in the fat in which the chicken was cooked, and fry gently without colouring. Meanwhile, slice the mushrooms, add them to the pan, and continue frying until they are tender. Pour in the wine, and add the chopped tomatoes or the tomato purée and the stock. Stir until well blended, then simmer gently for 10 minutes. Chop the herbs and add most of them to the sauce. Season to taste.

Pour the sauce over the chicken, sprinkle with the remaining herbs, and serve very hot.

CHICKEN WITH WALNUTS

4 helpings

4 × 15ml spoons/4 tablespoons
  cooking oil
200g/7oz shelled walnuts (whole *or*
  pieces)
4 whole chicken breasts
15g/½oz cornflour

a pinch of salt
a pinch of sugar
2–3 × 15ml spoons/2–3
  tablespoons soy sauce
200ml/8fl oz water
100g/4oz button mushrooms

GARNISH

fingers of toast

Heat the oil in a heavy-bottomed saucepan. Fry the walnuts gently in the oil for 2–3 minutes until golden-brown. Remove them, and drain on soft kitchen paper.

Skin and dice the chicken breasts. Fry the meat in the pan, turning gently until light golden on all sides. Mix the cornflour, salt, sugar, soy sauce and water to a smooth paste, and add the mixture to the pan. Slice the mushrooms and add them. Cook all these ingredients together very gently for about 10 minutes or until the meat is just tender. Stir the mixture during cooking, to prevent it sticking to the bottom of the pan. Remove from the heat, stir in the walnuts, and serve immediately. Garnish with fingers of toast.

THE WALNUT.

CHICKEN À LA KING

4 helpings

350–500g/¾–1lb cooked chicken
  meat
1 red pepper
175g/6oz button mushrooms
250g/8oz long-grain rice
50g/2oz butter

4 × 15ml spoons/4 tablespoons
  whisky
salt and freshly ground black
  pepper
a pinch of garlic powder
200ml/8fl oz double cream
1 egg yolk

Dice the chicken meat and put to one side. De-seed the pepper and slice it thinly. Trim and slice the mushrooms. Boil the rice for 12–15 minutes until tender, drain thoroughly, and keep hot.

Melt 25g/1oz of the butter in a frying pan and, when foaming, add the pepper and fry quickly for 2–3 minutes. Stir in the mushrooms, and cook gently for another 2 minutes. Put to one side. In a second pan, melt the remaining butter, add the diced chicken meat, and fry gently, turning as required, until well heated through. Pour on the whisky, set alight, and shake the pan to distribute the flames. When they die down, season the chicken well with salt, pepper, and garlic powder, and simmer until nearly all of the juices have evaporated. Stir in most of the cream, and bring gently to boiling point, stirring all the time. Blend the egg yolk into the remaining cream, and add a little of the cooking liquid from the pepper and mushrooms. Add the pepper and the mushrooms to the chicken, then stir in the yolk and cream. Re-heat gently without boiling until the sauce thickens a little. Pile on to a warmed serving dish, and surround with a ring of the rice. Serve hot.

Chicken Chasseur

DEVILLED CHICKEN

1 helping

1 poussin *or* chicken joint
salt and pepper
a pinch of ground ginger
a pinch of mustard powder

1 × 5ml spoon/1 teaspoon chopped parsley
1 × 5ml spoon/1 teaspoon chopped shallot
1 × 10ml spoon/1 dessertspoon cooking oil

Split the poussin, if used, along the back, open it out, and skewer it into a neat flattish shape. Season to taste with salt, pepper, ginger and mustard, and sprinkle the parsley and shallot over it. Allow to stand for about 1 hour, turning occasionally so that the meat absorbs the varous flavours. Brush with oil. Grill for 20–30 minutes or until tender, turning 2 or 3 times while cooking so that the outside is lightly browned. Serve very hot.

GINGER.

CHICKEN CASSEROLE

6 helpings

1 chicken *or* 6 small chicken joints
salt and pepper
25g/1oz flour
125g/5oz streaky bacon, without rinds

50g/2oz mushrooms
25g/1oz shallots
50g/2oz butter *or* fat
500ml/1 pint chicken stock

Joint the chicken. Season the flour, and dip the joints in it. Cut the bacon into strips 1.25cm/½ inch wide, slice the mushrooms, and skin and chop the shallots. Heat the fat in a flameproof casserole and fry the bacon, mushrooms, and shallots gently. Add the chicken joints and fry them until golden on all sides, turning them as required.

Add enough hot stock just to cover the chicken pieces. Simmer for 1–1½ hours or until tender. Re-season if required. Serve from the casserole.

Opposite, from the back, clockwise:
Poultry Hot Pot (page 113),
Chicken à la King (page 107) and
Chicken with Walnuts (page 107)

BRAISED CHICKEN WITH PARSLEY

4 helpings

50g/2oz parsley sprigs
100g/4oz butter
salt and pepper

2 spring chickens
150ml/6fl oz water
275ml/11fl oz double cream

GARNISH

lemon wedges

parsley sprigs

Cut the stalks off the parsley sprigs and chop the leaves coarsely. Soften 50g/2oz of the butter, season, and mix with half of the parsley. Place half the mixture in the body of each bird. Melt the remaining butter in a large pan, put the chickens in the pan, and brown them lightly all over. Add the water, cover, and cook gently for 40 minutes or until tender. Remove the chickens and halve them. Put in a serving dish and keep hot. Add the cream to the stock in the pan and cook over low heat, stirring until the sauce is smooth. Add the remaining parsley, and re-season if required. Pour the sauce over the chicken and garnish with lemon wedges and extra parsley sprigs.

Note If spring chickens are not available, use 1 roasting chicken, stuff it with the butter and parsley mixture, and cut it into quarters after cooking. Allow 10–15 minutes extra cooking time.

CHICKEN BRAISED WITH CHESTNUTS

4–6 helpings

400g/13oz chestnuts
1 small chicken
25g/1oz butter
1 × 15ml spoon/1 tablespoon olive
  oil *or* other good vegetable oil

125ml/¼ pint soy sauce
425 ml/17fl oz water
4 slices ginger root
2 spring onions
a pinch of salt

Remove the shells and skins of the chestnuts. Wipe the chicken and halve it. Cut each half into 4 pieces without removing any bones. Heat the butter and oil in a saucepan and fry the chicken until golden-brown. Add the soy sauce and water, and bring just to the boil. Remove the pan from the heat. Mince or grate the ginger and chop the onions. Add them to the saucepan with the skinned chestnuts and salt. Cover, and simmer for 1 hour or until the chicken is tender and the chestnuts have broken up and are thickening the sauce.

Ragoût of Chicken

1 chicken
1 onion
125g/5oz ham *or* bacon
50g/2oz butter

50g/2oz flour
500ml/1 pint chicken stock
salt and pepper

Joint the chicken. Skin and slice the onion. Dice the ham or bacon. Melt the butter in a saucepan and fry the joints in it until lightly browned; them remove and keep hot. Fry the sliced onion lightly in the same fat. Sprinkle in the flour and brown it slowly. Add the stock, season carefully, and stir until boiling. Replace the joints in the sauce, add the diced ham or bacon, cover with a tight-fitting lid, and cook gently for 1 hour or until the chicken is tender. Re-season if required.

Serve the chicken with the sauce poured over it.

Braised Chicken with Parsley

CHICKEN CASSEROLE WITH LEMON

6 helpings

6 chicken joints *or* 3 chicken
  quarters
salt and pepper
50g/2oz butter
1 × 15ml spoon/1 tablespoon oil
1 medium-sized onion
1 lemon

4 × 15ml spoons/4 tablespoons
  plain flour
250ml/½ pint chicken stock
2–3 bay leaves
1 × 5ml spoon/1 teaspoon caster
  sugar

Halve the chicken quarters, if used. Season the joints well with salt and pepper. Heat the butter and oil in a frying pan, and fry the joints until golden-brown all over. Transfer to a casserole.

Skin and slice the onion and slice the lemon. Put the onion in the frying pan and cook gently for about 5 minutes until tender. Sprinkle in the flour and cook for 1 minute. Blend in the stock and bring to the boil, stirring all the time. Add the sliced lemon, bay leaves, sugar, and salt and pepper to taste. Pour into the casserole and cover. Cook in a fairly hot oven, 190°C/375°F/Gas 5, for about 1 hour until the chicken is tender. Remove the casserole lid 5 minutes before the end of the cooking time.

BOILED FOWL.

CHICKEN WITH RICE

4 helpings

1 chicken *or* 4 chicken quarters
chicken giblets *or* 2 chicken stock
  cubes
2 × 15ml spoons/2 tablespoons oil
40g/1½oz butter
250g/8oz button onions

100g/4oz button mushrooms
1 bay leaf
50ml/2fl oz dry white wine
200g/7oz canned red peppers
175g/6oz long-grained rice
salt and pepper

GARNISH

chopped parsley

If using a whole chicken, cut into quarters. Cook the giblets in 1 litre/2 pints of water for 40 minutes, or make stock with the cubes. Put the oil and 25g/1oz of the butter in a large pan, add the chicken, and brown gently all over. Remove to a plate. Prepare the onions and mushrooms. Place them in the pan with the oil, bay leaf, wine, and 150ml/6fl oz of the stock. Cover, and cook for 15 minutes. Remove, measure the stock, and make up to 500ml/1 pint with the remaining stock.

Drain the peppers and cut them into strips. Heat the remaining 15g/½ oz butter in a frying pan and cook the rice in it gently for about 2 minutes. Add the onions, mushrooms, stock, wine and peppers. Season well. Place in a casserole, arrange the chicken on top, cover and cook in a moderate oven, 180°C/350°F/Gas 4, for 1 hour, by which time most of the stock will have been absorbed. Arrange the rice on a heated serving dish with the chicken on top and sprinkle with parsley.

POULTRY HOT POT

4–6 helpings

1 boiling fowl with giblets
3 rashers streaky bacon, without
   rinds
salt and pepper

nutmeg
2 onions
2 carrots
275ml/11fl oz chicken stock
3 × 10ml spoons/3 dessertspoons
   flour

GARNISH

2 × 15ml spoons/2 tablespoons
   chopped parsley

Joint the fowl and remove the skin. Place the joints, with the liver
and heart, in a casserole or saucepan with a tight-fitting lid. Cut the
bacon into strips, and add with the salt, pepper, and nutmeg.
Prepare and dice the onions and carrots, and add with the stock.
Cover, then either cook in a fairly hot oven, 190–200°C/375–
400°F/Gas 5–6, or simmer for about 2–2½ hours until tender.
Blend the flour with a little water, add some of the chicken stock,
and return to the pan. Stir it in, and cook until thickened. Serve
sprinkled with parsley.

   Boiled rice makes a good accompaniment.

Chicken Casserole with Lemon

HINDLE WAKES

6 helpings

1 × 1.5kg/3lb chicken
350ml/14fl oz chicken stock

grated rind and juice of ½ lemon
a blade of mace (optional)

STUFFING

175g/6oz prunes
50g/2oz onion
125g/5oz soft white breadcrumbs
1 × 5ml spoon/1 teaspoon dried
   mixed herbs

50g/2oz shredded suet
1 × 15ml spoon/1 tablespoon
   Demerara sugar
salt and pepper
1 × 15ml spoon/1 tablespoon malt
   vinegar

GARNISH

6 soaked prunes (see Method)

lemon slices
parsley (optional)

Make the stuffing first. Put the prunes in a basin, cover with cold water, and leave to soak overnight. Reserving 6 for the garnish, stone and chop the rest. Skin the onion and chop it finely. Mix it with the prunes, breadcrumbs, mixed herbs, suet, sugar, salt, and pepper. Sprinkle the mixture with the vinegar and mix together. Use the stuffing to fill the body cavity of the chicken.

Truss the chicken and place it in a large saucepan or flameproof casserole. Bring the stock to the boil, add the lemon rind and juice, and a blade of mace. Pour the stock over the chicken. Bring to the boil, reduce the heat, cover, and simmer for 1½ hours until tender. Drain, and garnish with the reserved prunes and lemon slices. Arrange in lines along the back of the chicken, using cocktail sticks to secure the garnish. Parsley sprigs can also be used. Serve with the stuffing and hot lemon stock.

CHICKEN WITH CURRIED RICE

4–6 helpings

1 chicken with giblets
1 carrot
2 sticks celery
1 litre/2 pints (approx) chicken
   stock *or* water
1 blade of mace
6 black peppercorns

150g/5oz long-grain rice
2 large mild onions
100g/4oz butter
1 × 15ml spoon/1 tablespoon curry
   paste
salt and pepper
50g/2oz small onions *or* shallots

Place the chicken in a large saucepan with the giblets. Slice the carrot and celery, and add them to the pan with enough stock or water to cover the chicken. Add the mace and peppercorns, and cover with a lid. Simmer gently for 2 hours or until the bird is tender. Drain well. Reserve the stock.

Strip the flesh from the chicken, and slice it. Wash and drain the rice. Skin and slice the large onions. Heat 50g/2oz of the butter in a pan and fry the onions until lightly browned. Add the curry paste, mix well, and fry gently for 2–3 minutes. Add the rice and 750ml/1½ pints of the reserved stock. Season to taste, cover, and simmer for 15–30 minutes until the rice is tender and the stock is absorbed. When ready, remove the rice from the heat, and keep warm.

Heat the remaining butter in a frying pan and add the chicken pieces; fry gently until browned on all sides. Leave the butter in the pan. Add the chicken to the rice mixture and cook slowly until the rice is heated through again. Stir in a little more stock if necessary, and re-season if required. Place on a serving dish and keep hot. Skin and slice the small onions or shallots into rings. Fry quickly in the butter used for the chicken, and pile on top of the rice. Serve very hot.

CHICKEN WITH CUCUMBER SAUCE

4–6 helpings

1 chicken
1 lemon
1 bay leaf
salt and pepper
1 small onion

1 cucumber
25g/1oz butter
25g/1oz plain flour
2 × 15ml spoons/2 tablespoons
   single cream

GARNISH

1 × 15ml spoon/1 tablespoon
  chopped parsley

Place the chicken in a large pan with just enough water to cover it. Pare the lemon rind thinly and add to the pan with the bay leaf, salt, and pepper to taste. Bring to the boil, cover, and simmer for 1½–2 hours until the chicken is tender. Skin and chop the onion. Dice the cucumber. Lift the chicken from the pan, cool slightly, and strip away the skin. Strain 250ml/½ pint stock from the pan for the sauce. Return the chicken to the pan and keep hot.

Melt the butter in another pan, add the onion and cucumber, and cook for 1 minute. Stir in the flour, gradually blend in the stock, and simmer gently for 10–15 minutes. Cool slightly. Squeeze a little juice from the lemon, and add to the sauce with the cream and salt and pepper to taste.

Lift the chicken on to a serving dish and coat with sauce. Sprinkle with parsley.

Chicken with Cucumber Sauce

CURRIED CHICKEN SALAD

6–8 helpings

1 large cooked chicken
150ml/6fl oz mayonnaise
25g/1oz curry powder

500g/1lb (approx) natural yoghurt
salt and pepper
paprika

GARNISH

parsley sprigs

thin green pepper rings

Remove the cooked meat from the bones. Take off any skin or fat, and cut into small pieces. Mix the mayonnaise with the curry powder, stir in the yoghurt, and season to taste. Mix half the sauce with the turkey or chicken, arrange on a serving dish, and spoon the remaining sauce over. Sprinkle with a little paprika and garnish with the parsley and pepper rings.

PARSLEY.

CHICKEN MAYONNAISE

6 helpings

1 cooked chicken *or* 6 cooked
   chicken joints

275ml/11fl oz aspic jelly
425ml/17fl oz mayonnaise

GARNISH

pickled walnuts

pieces of red and green pepper

Joint the whole chicken, if used; remove the skin, excess fat, and as much bone as possible, and trim the joints to a neat shape. Melt the aspic jelly. When almost cool, blend 150ml/6fl oz of it carefully into the mayonnaise. Beat well to blend thoroughly. Place the pieces of chicken on a wire cooling rack, and when the sauce is a good coating consistency, coat the pieces, using a large spoon. Cut the pickled nuts and the pieces of red and green pepper into attractive shapes for garnishing, dry well on soft kitchen paper, and stick on the chicken with dabs of half-set mayonnaise. Melt the remaining aspic jelly again if necessary; cool until it is on the point of setting, and use to coat the chicken thinly.

CHAUDFROID OF CHICKEN

6 helpings

6 cooked chicken joints
125ml/¼ pint aspic jelly
375ml/¾ pint mayonnaise

lettuce leaves
3 sticks celery
2 hard-boiled eggs

GARNISH

stoned olives *or* gherkins

tomato wedges *or* slices

Remove the skin, excess fat, and bones from the chicken joints, keeping the pieces in neat shapes. Melt the aspic jelly, and leave to cool. Just before it reaches setting point, while still tepid, add three-quarters of the mayonnaise, and whisk in. Blend to a smooth consistency. Place the chicken joints on a wire cooling tray and coat with the mayonnaise sauce as soon as it reaches a good coating consistency. Arrange the lettuce leaves on a serving dish and place the chicken joints on top. Prepare and chop the celery, slice the eggs, and arrange these round the chicken. Spoon the remaining mayonnaise over the celery and egg. Garnish with the olives or gherkins and the tomatoes.

Chaudfroid of Chicken

TURKEY

ROAST TURKEY WITH CHESTNUTS

1 turkey
salt and pepper
1kg/2 lb chestnuts
275ml/11fl oz stock
50g/2oz butter

1 egg
single cream *or* milk
500g/1lb sausage-meat
2–3 slices fat bacon
fat for basting

Season the turkey inside with salt and pepper, but do not truss it. Remove the shells and skins of the chestnuts. Stew them in the stock for 1 hour, then drain and chop or sieve them. Melt the butter and beat the egg, and add both to the chestnuts with seasoning and enough cream or milk to moisten the mixture. Fill the neck end of the bird with this chestnut stuffing, and the body of the bird with seasoned sausage-meat or basic forcemeat. Truss, and cover the bird with bacon. Roast for 15–20 minutes in a hot oven, 220°C/425°F/Gas 7, then reduce to moderate, 180°C/350°F/Gas 4, and cook for 20 minutes per 500g/1lb turkey weight plus 20 minutes, until tender. Baste well. Remove the bacon towards the end of the cooking time to allow the breast to brown. Remove the trussing string, and transfer the bird to a warmed serving dish.

Serve gravy separately.

TURKEY FRITTERS

— *4 helpings* —

400g/13oz sliced cold cooked
    turkey
50g/2oz ham *or* boiled bacon
1 egg

50g/2oz soft white breadcrumbs
2 × 5ml spoons/2 teaspoons
    chopped parsley
oil *or* fat for deep frying

Cut the turkey into neat pieces. Mince the ham or bacon very finely. Beat the egg until liquid. Mix together the minced ham, breadcrumbs, and parsley. Dip the turkey in the beaten egg and coat with the breadcrumb mixture. Press the coating on firmly. Heat the fat to 175–180°C/347–356°F, and fry the fritters until golden-brown. Drain and serve immediately.

MUSTARD.

DEVILLED TURKEY

4 helpings

2 cold cooked turkey legs
2 × 15ml spoons/2 tablespoons
   made English mustard

salt
a few grains Cayenne pepper
chilled pats of butter (optional)

Cut the legs in half at the joints. Score the flesh with lengthways slits cut down to the bone. Rub with the mustard, pressing it well into the slits. Season lightly with the salt and Cayenne pepper. Grill over moderate heat, turning as required, until crisp and brown. Top each joint with a pat of butter if liked, and serve very hot.

Roast Turkey with Chestnuts

TURKEY WINGS IN GINGER SAUCE

8 turkey wings
salt and pepper

flour for dredging
oil for shallow frying

SAUCE

juice of ½ lemon
4 × 15ml spoons/4 tablespoons
chopped stem ginger in syrup

2 × 15ml spoons/2 tablespoons
medium-dry sherry
25g/1oz butter

Remove and discard the pinions from the wings. Skin the wings by holding them firmly in soft kitchen paper or a cloth, and peeling off the skin. Season the flour with salt and pepper. Roll the wings in the flour. Heat the oil in a frying pan to a depth of 1.25cm/½ inch. Fry them gently, turning as required, until tender and golden-brown on both sides. This will take about 17–20 minutes. Remove from the pan, drain on soft kitchen paper, and keep hot while making the sauce.

Put the lemon juice, stem ginger, sherry, and butter in a small saucepan, and bring to the boil. Place the turkey wings on a heated serving platter and pour the sauce over them.

Serve with buttered noodles or plain boiled rice.

CASSEROLE OF TURKEY LEGS

2 turkey thighs *or* drumsticks
flour for dredging
50g/2oz butter *or* margarine
1 × 15ml spoon/1 tablespoon
cooking oil
1 medium-sized onion

1 large clove of garlic
125g/5oz mushrooms
400g/13oz canned tomatoes
2 chicken stock cubes
2 × 5ml spoons/2 teaspoons dried
marjoram
salt and pepper

Sprinkle the turkey legs with flour. Heat the fat in a large flameproof casserole, add the oil, and when hot, put in the turkey joints. Fry gently, turning as required, until browned on all sides. Drain on soft kitchen paper, Skin and chop the onion, add to the fat remaining in the casserole, and fry gently for about 5 minutes, until softened. Skin, crush, and add the garlic. Quarter the mushrooms, and add to the pan with the tomatoes and their liquid. Add the crumbled stock cubes, marjoram, and seasoning to taste. Return the turkey joints to the casserole, cover, and simmer, or cook in a warm oven, 160°C/325°F/Gas 3, for 1½ hours or until the meat is very tender.

Remove the meat from the bones, and serve from the casserole.

BLANQUETTE OF TURKEY

4 helpings

1 small onion
turkey bones, raw *or* cooked
1 blade of mace
salt and pepper
600ml/1 pint water (approx)
40g/1½ oz butter

40g/1½ oz flour
350–450g/¾–1lb cooked turkey
    meat
a pinch of nutmeg
2 × 15ml spoons/2 tablespoons
    cream *or* top of milk
1 egg yolk

Skin and slice the onion. Place the turkey bones, onion, mace, and seasoning in a pan. Add about 600ml/1 pint water, cover the pan, and simmer for at least 1 hour. Strain, and reserve 450ml/¾ pint of the stock.

Melt the butter in a pan, stir in the flour, and cook for 2 minutes without browning. Gradually stir in the reserved stock. Bring to the boil, stirring all the time, and cook for 10 minutes. Dice the turkey meat. Add the nutmeg and turkey pieces to the sauce, and re-season if required. Heat thoroughly for about 20 minutes. Mix the cream or milk with the egg yolk, and stir in a little of the hot sauce. Return the mixture to the pan, and heat gently without boiling for about 5 minutes.

Serve hot with boiled rice.

Turkey Wings in Ginger Sauce

BRAISED TURKEY

12–14 helpings

1 turkey (5–6kg/10–12lb approx)
2 onions
2 carrots
1 leek
4 sticks celery
1 small turnip
2 rashers streaky bacon without
  rinds
100g/4oz butter *or* margarine

1.5 litres/3 pints chicken stock
125ml/¼ pint red wine
a pinch of dried thyme
1 bay leaf
6 parsley sprigs
salt and pepper
25g/1oz flour
2 × 15ml spoons/2 tablespoons
  double cream

GARNISH

chopped parsley

Choose a large pan which will hold the turkey, or halve the bird lengthways, and place each half in a large deep roasting tin. (In this case, divide the other ingredients equally between the tins.)

Prepare and chop all the vegetables and the bacon. Melt the butter or margarine in the pan, and fry the chopped vegetables and bacon, turning as required, until lightly browned all over. Add the turkey, pour the stock and wine over the bird, and add the herbs and seasoning. Cover tightly with a lid or foil, and simmer very gently for 3½–4 hours. (If cooking the halved bird in 2 tins, reduce the cooking time to 2–2½ hours.) Baste occasionally with the liquid in the pan while cooking.

When the bird is tender, remove it from the pan, and keep hot. Strain the remaining cooking liquid into a smaller pan. Discard the vegetables and herbs. Blend the flour to a smooth paste with a little cold water, and stir it into the stock in the pan. Place over gentle heat, and stir until the sauce thickens. Stir in the cream, and re-heat, but do not boil. Place the bird on a heated serving platter and sprinkle with chopped parsley. Serve the sauce separately.

Opposite, from the back, clockwise:
Turkey Salad (page 125),
Turkey Mousse (page 123) and
Deviled Turkey (page 119)

TURKEY MOUSSE

4 helpings

250g/8oz cooked turkey breast
  meat
275ml/11fl oz double cream
275ml/11fl oz chicken stock *or*
  broth with fat removed

1 × 15ml spoon/1 tablespoon
  gelatine
3 egg yolks
salt and pepper
4 × 10ml spoons/4 dessertspoons
  mayonnaise

GARNISH

watercress sprigs
small lettuce leaves

Remove any skin, gristle, and fat from the turkey. Mince the meat finely. Whip the cream until semi-stiff, then chill. Put 100ml/4fl oz of the stock or broth in a heatproof container, and sprinkle on the gelatine. Leave until softened. Meanwhile, beat the egg yolks lightly and stir into the rest of the stock or broth. Season if required, and cook gently in the top of a double boiler until the custard thickens. Remove from the heat, and turn into a chilled bowl. Dissolve the softened gelatine by standing the container in a pan of hot water. Stir until dissolved; then stir it into the egg custard, blending well. Blend the minced turkey meat in thoroughly. Stand the bowl in a basin of cold water or crushed ice, or chill until the mousse mixture begins to thicken at the edges. Fold in the chilled whipped cream and the mayonnaise at once. Turn into a wetted 1 litre/2 pint mould and chill until set. Turn out on to a platter, and garnish with watercress sprigs and small lettuce leaves.

SWEET AND SOUR TURKEY SALAD

4–5 helpings

250g/8oz canned pineapple rings
a pinch of salt
a pinch of pepper
a pinch of dry English mustard
a pinch of caster sugar
4 × 15ml spoons/4 tablespoons
  corn oil
1 × 5ml spoon/1 teaspoon soy
  sauce

1 × 15ml spoon/1 tablespoon cider
  vinegar
500g/1lb canned bean sprouts
250g/8oz cold cooked turkey
1 small green pepper
100g/4oz carrots
50g/2oz whole blanched almonds

Drain the juice from the pineapple and reserve 1 × 15ml spoon/1 tablespoon for the dressing. Put the salt, pepper, dry mustard, and sugar in a mixing bowl and add the corn oil. Blend together. Gradually add the reserved pineapple juice, the soy sauce and vinegar, and beat well. Drain the bean sprouts and add them to the dressing. Cut the turkey meat into pieces and add it to the bowl. Remove the membranes and seeds from the pepper and cut the flesh into thin strips. Scrape the carrot, and cut into thin strips. Add both to the bowl. Toast the almonds lightly. Cut the pineapple into segments and stir into the salad with the almonds. Transfer to a salad bowl or dish. Chill before serving.

TURKEY SALAD

4 helpings

375g/12oz cold cooked turkey
1 hard-boiled egg
2 sticks celery
1 × 15ml spoon/1 tablespoon corn
  salad oil

1 × 15ml spoon/1 tablespoon
  vinegar
salt and pepper
6 × 15ml spoons/6 tablespoons
  mayonnaise
lettuce leaves

GARNISH

selection of gherkins, capers,
  anchovy fillets, radishes, and
  watercress

Cut the turkey into neat pieces. Separate the egg white and yolk. Chop the celery and egg white. Mix all these together with the corn oil, vinegar, and seasoning. Leave to stand for 1 hour. Stir in the mayonnaise. Sieve the egg yolk. Pile the turkey, celery and egg white on a bed of lettuce, sprinkle with the sieved yolk, and garnish as liked. Chill before serving.

ROAST TURKEY.

DUCK & GOOSE

DUCKLING IN RED WINE

4 helpings

1 duckling
salt and pepper
2 medium-sized onions
1 bay leaf
250ml/½ pint red wine
100g/4oz bacon
1 × 10ml spoon/1 dessertspoon
   cooking oil

400ml/16fl oz stock
1 medium-sized carrot
2 sticks celery
grated rind of 1 orange *or* lemon
100g/4oz button mushrooms

Cut the duckling into quarters and season well. Skin and chop the onions finely, and put into a bowl with the duck quarters, bay leaf, and red wine. Cover, and leave to marinate for 2 hours. Remove the duck portions from the wine and dry on soft kitchen paper; strain and reserve the liquid.

Chop the bacon. Heat the oil in a pan and cook the bacon gently for 3–4 minutes. Add the duckling and brown it all over. Drain well, and put in a casserole. Heat the stock and pour it into the casserole. Cook in a moderate oven, 180°C/350°F/Gas 4, for 15 minutes.

Meanwhile, prepare and slice the carrot and celery. Add to the casserole with the grated rind, mushrooms, and the reserved marinade. Cover, and cook for 1½–2 hours until tender. Skim off any surplus fat before serving.

Sweet and Sour Turkey Salad

ROAST GOOSE WITH FRUIT STUFFING AND RED CABBAGE

375g/12oz prunes
1 goose with giblets
1.5 litres/3 pints water
½ lemon

salt and pepper
500g/1lb cooking apples
1 × 15ml spoon/1 tablespoon
 redcurrant jelly

RED CABBAGE

1.5kg/3lb red cabbage
50g/2oz butter
50g/2oz Demerara sugar

75ml/3fl oz water
75ml/3fl oz malt or cider vinegar
salt and pepper

Soak the prunes overnight. Remove the giblets from the goose and simmer them in 1.5 litres/3 pints water until the stock is reduced by half. Put to one side. Weigh the goose and calculate the cooking time at 20 minutes for every 500g/1lb. Remove the excess fat usually found around the vent. Rinse the inside of the bird, then rub the skin with lemon. Season with salt and pepper. Remove the stones from the prunes and chop the flesh. Peel and core the apples and chop them roughly. Mix with the prunes and season to taste. Stuff into the body of the bird. Place in a very hot oven, 230°C/450°F/Gas 8, reduce the temperature immediately to moderate, 180°C/350°F/Gas 4, and cook for the calculated time.

Meanwhile, prepare the red cabbage. Shred finely. Melt the butter in a large flameproof casserole. Add the sugar and cabbage and stir well. Add the water, vinegar, and seasoning, cover and cook in the bottom of the oven for about 2 hours, stirring occasionally.

When the goose is cooked, drain off the excess fat, retaining the juices in the pan. Make a slightly thickened gravy using the reserved stock and the juices. Add the redcurrant jelly and stir until it melts.

Serve the gravy and red cabbage separately.

DUCK AND ORANGE CURRY

1 duck
salt
2 × 15ml spoons/2 tablespoons
 margarine or vegetable oil
2 large onions
2 cloves garlic
1 × 2.5ml spoon/½ teaspoon
 cardamom seeds
1 × 10ml spoon/1 dessertspoon
 finely chopped ginger root

1 × 5ml spoon/1 teaspoon cumin
1 × 5ml spoon/ teaspoon turmeric
1 × 10ml spoon/1 dessertspoon
 ground coriander
1 × 5cm/2 inch piece cinnamon
 bark
6 cloves
freshly ground black pepper
750ml/1½ pints unsweetened
 orange juice

Joint the duck into 4 or 6 pieces, removing any surplus fat. Season well with salt. Heat the margarine or oil, add the duck, and fry for 15–20 minutes, turning frequently. Remove the duck from the pan and put to one side. Skin and chop the onions and cloves of garlic, add them to the fat left in the pan, and fry until transparent. Add all the spices and the orange juice and bring to the boil, stirring all the time. Replace the duck in the pan, cover, and simmer for 1¼–1½ hours. Season with a little extra salt if required.

Serve with rice and other curry accompaniments.

THE OLIVE.

DUCK WITH GREEN OLIVES

4–5 helpings

500ml/1 pint water
giblets of 1 duck
2 carrots
2 medium-sized onions
bouquet garni
salt and pepper

1 duck
2 × 15ml spoons/2 tablespoons
   goose, duck *or* chicken fat
2 slices stale white bread
24 stuffed green olives
3 small carrots

Put the water in a saucepan with the duck giblets but reserve the liver (this can be used for another dish). Cut up the carrots and onions roughly and add them to the pan with the bouquet garni and seasoning to taste. Simmer uncovered for about 40 minutes to obtain about 375ml/¾ pint well-flavoured stock. Put to one side.

Meanwhile, season the inside of the duck. Heat the fat in a heavy flameproof casserole, put in the duck, and brown it on all sides. Reduce the heat, cover the casserole, and cook slowly for 15 minutes. Remove the duck, joint it, and return the joints to the casserole. Grate or crumble the bread, sprinkle it over the duck, and strain the stock over the dish. Plunge the olives into boiling water for 1 minute, then add them to the casserole. Slice the small carrots thinly, and add them also. Cover the casserole, place over low heat, and simmer for 45 minutes.

Serve with boiled rice.

Roast Goose with Fruit Stuffing and Red Cabbage

DUCK IN ORANGE AND CLARET

4–5 helpings

1 cold roast duck
25g/1oz butter
1 onion
25g/1oz flour

500ml/1 pint beef stock
1 orange
100ml/4fl oz claret
salt and pepper

Carve the duck ready for serving. Melt the butter in a saucepan, skin and chop the onion finely, and fry it in the butter. Stir in the flour and cook gently until brown. Add the stock, stir until boiling, and simmer for 10 minutes. Pare the rind of the orange, cut it into very thin strips, and squeeze out the juice from the orange. Add the rind to the sauce with the orange juice, claret, and pieces of duck. Season to taste. Simmer very gently for 30 minutes. Arrange the meat on a serving dish and pour the sauce over it.

ROAST DUCK.

DUCK OR GOOSE ON CROÛTES

4 helpings

375g/12oz trimmings of roast goose
  or duck
2 onions
50g/2oz butter
25g/1oz flour
500ml/1 pint beef stock
2 cloves

1 blade of mace
6 allspice berries
6 small mushrooms
salt and pepper
8 croûtes fried bread 8.75cm/3½
  inches in diameter

Cut the meat into neat pieces. Skin and chop the onions finely, melt the butter in a saucepan, and fry the onions until lightly browned. Stir in the flour and cook slowly until nut-brown. Stir in the stock and boil for 10 minutes. Tie the spices in muslin and add with the mushrooms to the pan. Season to taste, and simmer gently for 20 minutes. Arrange the pieces of meat neatly on the croûtes, remove the spices from the sauce, re-season if required, and pour the sauce over the meat.

Serve apple sauce separately.

SALMI OF DUCK

4 helpings

1 Spanish onion
1 duck *or* trimmings from 2 cold
   roast ducks
fat for basting
40g/1½oz butter

25g/1oz flour
350ml/14fl oz beef stock
12 stoned green olives
salt and pepper

If using a whole duck, skin and slice the onion into a roasting tin, put the prepared duck on top, baste with hot fat and roast in a fairly hot oven, 190–200°C/375–400°F/Gas 5–6, for 1–1½ hours or until tender.

Melt the butter in a small saucepan, add the flour, and cook slowly until the flour browns. Stir in the stock and simmer until thick. Keep warm. Remove the trussing string from the roast duck and cut it into small joints. Add either the freshly roasted or the cold duck to the sauce with the olives; season, and re-heat thoroughly. Sieve the onion or chop it finely, and add to the duck. Drain off the fat from the roasting tin and add the sediment to the sauce.

The salmi can be served on croûtes of fried bread with the sauce and olives poured over them.

Salmi of Duck

DUCK WITH GREEN PEAS

4–5 helpings

1kg/2lb fresh peas
12 button *or* spring onions
250g/8oz rashers streaky bacon
50g/2oz butter
1 duck

425ml/17fl oz chicken stock
bouquet garni
salt and pepper
sugar
1 small round lettuce (optional)

Shell the peas and put to one side. Prepare the onions, and parboil them with the bacon. Drain. In an ovenproof casserole or saucepan large enough to hold the duck, melt the butter, add the onions and bacon, and toss quickly until light brown in colour. Remove from the pan. Put the duck in the pan and brown it well all over, then remove it.

Put a third of the stock into the pan and boil down to half its quantity, then add the remainder of the stock with the duck, onions, bacon, peas, and bouquet garni. Season lightly with salt and pepper and a pinch of sugar. Bring to the boil, then cover the pan and cook in a fairly hot oven, 190°C/375°F/Gas 5, for about 45 minutes. Baste from time to time.

Remove the duck and place on a serving dish; surround with the peas, onions, and bacon. Reduce the cooking liquor by boiling, then pour it over the duck.

A quartered lettuce may be added to the duck and peas when cooking; in this case, cut and serve the duck in quarters, and garnish with lettuce leaves as well as the other vegetables.

MEAT

·

HOW TO BUY MEAT ECONOMICALLY.—If the housekeeper is not very particular as to the precise joints to cook for dinner, there is oftentimes an opportunity for her to save as much money in her purchases of meat as will pay for the bread to eat with it. It often occurs, for instance that the butcher may have a superfluity of certain joints, and these he would be glad to get rid of at a reduction of sometimes as much as 1*d.* or 1½*d*, per lb., and thus, in a joint of 8 or 9 lbs., will be saved enough to buy 2 quartern loaves. It frequently happens with many butchers, that, in consequence of a demand for legs and loins of mutton, they have only shoulders left, and these they will be glad to sell at a reduction.

Isabella Beeton 1861

Left: *Mrs Beeton's Oxford Sausages (page 157)* and *Carbonnade of Beef (page 134)*
Below: *Fricasée of Lamb (page 142)*

BEEF

STEAK DIANE

4 helpings

4 minute, fillet *or* rump steaks
1 small onion
75g/3oz unsalted butter
grated rind and juice of 1 lemon
1×5ml spoon/1 teaspoon caster
    sugar

Worcestershire sauce
1×15ml spoon/1 tablespoon
    chopped parsley
2×15ml spoons/2 tablespoons
    brandy

In the kitchen, wipe the steaks and trim off any excess fat. Beat them flat with a cutlet bat or rolling-pin until they are no more than 6mm/¼inch thick. Skin the onion and chop it finely. Take all the ingredients to the table.

At the table, melt 50g/2oz of the butter in a large, heavy-based frying pan and fry the onion for about 5 minutes until soft. Remove the onion from the pan and keep warm on a plate. Raise the heat under the pan. Using the remaining butter, fry 2 steaks at a time over high heat for 1 minute on each side. Remove from the pan and keep warm. Return the onions to the pan, and add the lemon rind and juice, the sugar, and a few drops of Worcestershire sauce. Stir in the parsley and cook lightly. Warm the brandy. Put the steaks into the pan and flame with the warmed brandy. Serve immediately, with the sauce spooned over them, and with chipped potatoes, grilled mushrooms and/or tomatoes.

STEAKS WITH MUSTARD SAUCE

4 helpings

4 fillet *or* sirloin steaks
freshly ground pepper
25g/1oz unsalted butter
2×15ml spoons/2 tablespoons oil
150ml/6fl oz soured cream

1×5ml spoon/1 teaspoon lemon
    juice
2×5ml spoons/2 teaspoons French
    mustard
salt

Wipe the steaks and trim off any excess fat. Beat each steak lightly on both sides with a cutlet bat or rolling pin. Season with pepper. Heat the butter and oil in a heavy-based frying pan. When hot, put in the steaks and fry quickly on both sides for 6–8 minutes according to requirement. Lift out the steaks, transfer them to a warmed serving dish, and keep hot. Stir the soured cream into the juices in the pan and cook gently, without boiling. Stir in the lemon juice, mustard, and salt to taste. Pour the mustard sauce over the steaks and serve at once.

POTATOES.

HOT BEEF PIE

6 helpings

750g/1½lb stewing steak
   (chuck, blade *or* neck)
3 medium-sized onions
3 large carrots

1kg/2lb potatoes
salt and pepper
beef stock *or* water as required

Wipe the meat and trim of any excess fat. Cut the meat into 2.5cm/1 inch cubes. Prepare the vegetables. Slice the onions and carrots thinly, and cut the potatoes into slices about 6mm/¼ inch thick. Arrange the meat, onion, carrot, and potato slices in layers in a 2 litre/4 pint casserole, finishing with a neat layer of potatoes. Season with salt and pepper. Three-quarters cover the meat and vegetables with stock or water (add more during cooking if the dish seems dry). Cover the pan with a tight-fitting lid and cook in a warm oven, 160°C/325°F/Gas 3, for 2 hours.

Uncover 30 minutes before the end of the cooking time to allow the top layer of potato to brown. Serve from the casserole.

Steak Diane

BEEF À LA MODE

1kg/2lb rump of beef
25g/1oz butter *or* dripping
10 button onions
25g/1oz plain flour
750ml/1½ pints beef stock

salt and pepper
2 rashers streaky bacon, without rinds
2 medium-sized carrots

MARINADE

1 small onion
100ml/4fl oz claret
juice of ½ lemon

2 cloves
salt and pepper
bouquet garni

Wipe, trim, and tie the meat into a neat shape if necessary.

Make the marinade first. Skin and chop the onion finely. Mix all the ingredients for the marinade, put in the meat, and leave to stand for 2 hours, basting frequently. Drain the beef thoroughly, and strain and reserve the marinade.

Heat the butter or dripping in a large stewpan and fry the meat in the hot fat, turning it until browned on all sides. Skin the button onions and fry at the same time, turning them so that they brown evenly. Remove the beef and onions and put to one side. Stir the flour into the fat in the pan and cook until browned. Gradually add the stock and the marinade and stir until boiling. Replace the meat and onions. Season to taste. Cover the top of the meat with the bacon. Slice the carrots thinly, then add them to the pan. Cover with a tight-fitting lid and cook gently for 2½ hours, stirring occasionally, or transfer to an ovenproof dish, cover, and cook in a warm oven, 160°C/325°F/Gas 3, for 2 hours. When tender, transfer the meat to a warmed serving dish and keep hot. Strain the liquid in the stewpan or casserole, and pour it over the meat.

Note If liked, the bacon, onions, and carrots can be served with the meat although they will have given up most of their food value during the long, slow cooking.

CARBONNADE OF BEEF

750g/1½lb stewing steak (chuck, blade, skirt *or* thin flank)
50g/2oz dripping
2 large onions
1 clove of garlic
1×15ml spoon/1 tablespoon plain flour
250ml/½ pint beef stock *or* water
375ml/¾ pint brown ale
salt and pepper
bouquet garni
a pinch of grated nutmeg

a pinch of light soft brown sugar
1×5ml spoon/1 teaspoon red wine vinegar
6 thin slices from a French bâton loaf
1×15ml spoon/1 tablespoon French mustard *or* 1×15ml spoon/1 tablespoon English mustard mixed with vinegar to taste

Wipe the meat and trim off any excess fat. Cut the meat into 2.5–3.75cm/1–1½ inch cubes. Heat the dripping in a large pan. Fry the meat quickly until brown on all sides. Transfer to a casserole and keep warm. Skin and slice the onions and fry them in the fat in the pan until lightly browned. Skin and crush the garlic, add it to the onions and fry gently for 1 minute. Pour off any excess fat. Sprinkle the flour over the onion and garlic and cook, stirring until just beginnning to brown. Gradually stir in the stock or water, and the ale. Add the salt and pepper, bouquet garni, nutmeg, sugar, and vinegar. Heat to boiling point and pour the liquid over the meat in the casserole. Cover, and cook in a warm oven, 160°C/325°F/Gas 3, for 1½–2 hours.

When cooked, remove the bouquet garni, spread the slices of bread with mustard, and press them well down into the gravy. Return the casserole, uncovered, to the oven, for about 15 minutes to allow the bread to brown slightly. Serve from the casserole.

MRS BEETON'S ROAST RIBS OF BEEF

6–8 helpings

2.5kg/5lb forerib of beef
flour for dredging

50–75g/2–3oz clarified dripping
(see **Note**)
salt and pepper

GARNISH

shredded horseradish

Ask the butcher to trim the thin ends of the rib bones so that the joint will stand upright. Wipe the meat but do not salt it. Dredge it lightly with flour. Melt 50g/2oz dripping in a roasting tin and brush some of it over the meat. Put the meat in the tin and roast it in a very hot oven, 230°C/450°F/Gas 8, for 10 minutes. Baste well, reduce heat to moderate, 180°C/350°F/Gas 4, and continue to roast for 1¾ hours for rare meat, or 2¼ hours for well-done meat. Baste frequently during cooking, using extra dripping if required.

When cooked, salt the meat lightly. Transfer the joint to a warmed serving dish and keep hot. Pour off almost all the fat in the roasting tin, leaving the sediment. Pour in enough water to make a thin gravy, then heat to boiling point, stirring all the time. Taste, and season with salt and pepper. Strain the gravy into a warmed gravy-boat. Garnish the dish with 1 or 2 small heaps of shredded horseradish.

Note To clarify dripping, put the dripping into a large saucepan and add about the same volume of cold water. Heat very gently until the water begins to boil, removing the scum as it rises. Allow to simmer for about 5 minutes, then strain into a bowl and leave to cool and solidify. Remove the fat in one piece, dry it on soft kitchen paper and scrape away the sediment from underneath. Heat the fat very slowly until all bubbling ceases, to drive off any water.

Mrs Beeton's Roast Ribs of Beef

IRISH SPICED BEEF

(for Christmas)

6–8 helpings

3kg/6lb lean boned joint of beef	3 carrots
1×5ml spoon/1 teaspoon ground allspice	3 medium-sized onions
1×5ml spoon/1 teaspoon ground cloves	a bundle of fresh mixed herbs *or* bouquet garni
	250ml/½ pint stout

SPICING MIXTURE

1×5ml spoon/1 teaspoon ground cloves	3×15ml spoons/3 tablespoons soft light brown sugar
6 blades mace	2×5ml spoons/2 teaspoons saltpetre
1×5ml spoon/1 teaspoon peppercorns	500g/1lb coarse salt
1×5ml spoon/1 teaspoon allspice	3 bay leaves
	1 clove of garlic

Make the spicing mixture first. Mix all the dry ingredients together, then pound in the bay leaves and garlic. Stand the meat in a large earthenware or glass dish, and rub the spicing mixture thoroughly all over it. Repeat every day for a week, taking the spicing mixture from the bottom of the dish. Turn the meat over twice. At the end of the week, wash the meat and tie it into a convenient shape for cooking.

Sprinkle the allspice and cloves over the meat. Prepare and chop the carrots and the onions. Make a bed of the vegetables and the herbs in a large saucepan. Put the meat on top. Barely cover with warm water, cover with a lid, and simmer gently for 5 hours. Add the stout for the last hour of the cooking time.

Serve hot or cold (At Christmas, the beef is usually served cold, in slices). To serve cold, remove the hot meat from the cooking liquid, and press between 2 dishes, with a weight on top, until cold.

MRS BEETON'S BOILED MARROW BONES

2 pieces of marrow bone per helping

marrow bones (150g/5oz each)	flour

Choose marrow bones from the leg or shin. Ask your butcher to saw them across into pieces 7.5cm/3 inches long, or do it yourself. Shape the thick ends by chopping them so that the bones will stand upright. Mix some flour to a stiff paste with water, and plaster this paste over the open end of each bone to seal in the marrow. Tie each bone in a floured cloth.

Stand the bones upright in a deep saucepan containing enough boiling water to come half-way up the bones. Cover the pan with a tight-fitting lid, reduce the heat, and simmer gently for about 1½ hours. Refill the pan with boiling water, if necessary. When cooked, remove the bones from the cloth and scrape off the paste. Fasten a paper napkin round each one and serve with a pointed teaspoon to extract the marrow.

Serve with Melba or hot dry toast and a seasoning of pepper.

SHEPHERD'S PIE

4–6 helpings

625g/1¼lb lean beef mince
2 medium-sized onions
25g/1oz dripping
1×15ml spoon/1 tablespoon flour
150ml/6fl oz strong beef stock
salt and freshly ground black
  pepper

750g/1½lb potatoes
a pinch of grated nutmeg
milk
1–2×15ml spoons/1–2 tablespoons
  butter (optional)
butter for greasing

Break up any lumps in the meat with a fork. Skin and slice the onions. Melt the dripping in a saucepan, and fry the onions until softened but not coloured. Stir in the flour, and cook gently for 1–2 minutes, stirring all the time. Gradually add the stock, without letting lumps form, and stir until boiling. Reduce the heat, and simmer for 2–3 minutes until the sauce thickens. Stir in the mince, cover the pan, and simmer for 20 minutes. Season well, replace the lid, and simmer for 10 minutes longer or until the mince is cooked through and tender.

Meanwhile, prepare the potatoes and boil them in salted water until tender. Mash them until smooth with a seasoning of salt, pepper and nutmeg, enough milk to make them creamy, and butter, if liked. Put the meat and sauce into a greased pie dish or shallow oven-to-table baking dish. Cover with the potato, smooth the top, then flick it up into small peaks or score a pattern on the surface with a fork. Bake for 10–15 minutes in a hot oven, 220°C/425°F/Gas 7, until browned on top. Serve hot.

Irish Spiced Beef

MEATBALLS IN SPICY SAUCE

4 helpings

1 small onion
1 small clove of garlic
400g/13oz raw minced beef
50g/2oz soft white breadcrumbs
2×15ml spoons/2 tablespoons
  chopped parsley

salt and pepper
2 eggs
3×15ml spoons/3 tablespoons
  cooking *or* olive oil

SPICY SAUCE

2×15ml spoons/2 tablespoons oil
2 small onions
1 stick of celery
2×15ml spoons/2 tablespoons
  concentrated tomato purée
1×15ml spoon/1 tablespoon
  Worcestershire sauce

Tabasco sauce
1×15ml spoon/1 tablespoon
  vinegar
1×5ml spoon/1 teaspoon made
  mustard
300ml/12fl oz water
salt and pepper

Make the sauce first. Heat the oil in a saucepan. Skin and chop the onions. Wash and chop the celery finely. Fry the onions and celery gently in the oil until softened. Add the tomato purée, and mix well. Stir in the Worcestershire and Tabasco sauces, the vinegar, mustard, and water. Season with salt and pepper. Heat to boiling point, reduce the heat, cover with a lid, and simmer for about 25 minutes.

Prepare the meatballs. Skin and chop the onion finely and skin and crush the garlic. Mix together the onion, garlic, meat, breadcrumbs, parsley, and seasoning. Beat the eggs until liquid and use to bind the meat mixture. Divide into sixteen pieces and shape into balls. Heat the oil in a frying pan. Add the meatballs and fry, turning frequently, until browned all over. Drain the excess oil and fat from the pan. Pour in the spicy sauce, cover the pan with a tight-fitting lid, and cook for about 45 minutes.

EXETER STEW

6 helpings

750g/1½lb chuck steak *or* blade *or*
  neck of beef
3×10ml spoons/3 dessertspoons
  dripping
3 medium-sized onions

3×15ml spoons/3 tablespoons
  plain flour
625ml/1¼ pints water
1×5ml spoon/1 teaspoon vinegar
salt and pepper

SAVOURY PARSLEY BALLS

100g/4oz plain flour
½×2.5ml spoon/¼ teaspoon
  baking powder
4½×15ml spoons/4½ tablespoons
  shredded suet
1×15ml spoon/1 tablespoon finely
  chopped parsley

1×2.5ml spoon/½ teaspoon dried
  mixed herbs
1×5ml spoon/1 teaspoon salt
1×2.5ml spoon/½ teaspoon
  ground pepper
1 egg *or* 3×15ml spoons/3
  tablespoons milk

Wipe the meat and trim off any excess fat. Cut the meat into 5cm/2 inch cubes. Heat the dripping in a stewpan and fry the meat and put to one side. Skin and slice the onions. Put them in the pan, and fry gently until light brown. Add the flour and cook, stirring until browned. Mix in the water and stir until boiling. Reduce the heat to simmering point. Add the vinegar and seasoning to taste. Return the meat, cover the pan, and simmer gently for 1½ hours.

To make the parsley balls, sift the flour and baking powder into a bowl. Add the suet, herbs, salt and pepper, and mix together. Beat the egg, if used, until liquid and bind the dry ingredients together with the beaten egg or milk to form a stiff dough. Divide the dough into 12 equal pieces and roll each into a ball.

Heat the stew to boiling point and drop in the balls. Reduce the heat and simmer for a further 30 minutes with the pan half-covered. Pile the meat in the centre of a warmed serving dish, pour the gravy over it and arrange the balls neatly round the base.

Opposite, from the back, clockwise:
Hot Beef Pie (page 133),
Shepherd's Pie (page 137) and
Exeter Stew (page 138)

LAMB

ROAST LEG OF LAMB

a leg of lamb *or* mutton   oil *or* fat for basting
salt and pepper

Weigh the leg joint to calculate the cooking time, allowing 20 minutes per 500g/1lb plus 20 minutes extra. Wipe the meat. Place the leg on a wire rack, if available, in a shallow roasting tin. Season the meat, and either pour over it a little oil or rub it with a little fat. Place the roasting tin in the oven, and cook in a very hot oven 230°C/450°F/Gas 8, for about 10 minutes to sear or brown the outside of the meat and seal in the juices. Reduce the temperature to fairly hot, 190°C/375°F/Gas 5, to finish the cooking.

  Transfer the cooked meat from the oven to a warmed meat dish, and keep hot. Prepare a gravy, if liked, from the sediment in the roasting tin.

  Serve with mint sauce.

BAKED LAMB OR MUTTON CUTLETS WITH MUSHROOMS

6 helpings

6 cutlets from best end of neck of   fat for greasing
  lamb *or* mutton   200g/7oz button mushrooms
salt and pepper   1 × 10ml spoon/1 dessertspoon oil
                                           or butter

Wipe and trim the cutlets neatly. Season the cutlets on both sides and place them in a single layer in a greased casserole or ovenproof dish. Clean the mushrooms and scatter them over the cutlets. Season to taste with salt and pepper, and sprinkle with oil or dot with pats of butter. Cover with a tight-fitting lid and bake in a cool oven, 150°C/300°F/Gas 2, for 1–1½ hours, until the cutlets are tender.

MUTTON CUTLETS.

LAMB OR MUTTON SHASHLIK

4 helpings

500g/1lb boned leg of lamb *or* mutton
50g/2oz butter
200g/7oz lean bacon

8 button onions
8 bay leaves
salt and pepper

Wipe the meat and trim off any excess fat. Cut the meat into 2.5cm/1 inch cubes. Heat 25g/1oz of the butter in a pan and brown the meat on all sides. Cut the bacon into slightly smaller cubes. Skin the onions and parboil them in slightly salted water for 3 minutes. Drain. Divide the meat, bacon, onions, and bay leaves into four portions and thread each portion on to a long skewer. Season with salt and pepper. Melt the remaining butter and brush it over the meat, bacon, and onions on the skewers. Grill under high heat, or over a charcoal fire, turning the skewers occasionally, for 8–10 minutes until the meat is well browned.

Serve with boiled rice.

Roast Leg of Lamb

FRICASSÉE OF LAMB

4–6 helpings

a breast of lamb
   (750g/1½lb approx)
1 medium-sized onion
50g/2oz dripping *or* lard *or*
   margarine
2 bay leaves
2 cloves

1 blade of mace
6 white peppercorns
salt and pepper
500ml/1 pint water
25g/1oz plain flour
500g/1lb creamed potatoes

GARNISH

1×10ml spoon/1 dessertspoon
   roughly chopped capers

Wipe the meat, bone it, if not already done by the butcher, and trim of any excess fat. Cut the meat into 5cm/2 inch squares. Skin and slice the onion. Melt the fat in a stewpan, add the meat, onion, bay leaves, cloves, mace, peppercorns, and salt and pepper to taste. Half cover the pan and cook very gently for about 30 minutes, stirring often. Meanwhile, heat the water to boiling point. Add it to the pan, and simmer, covered, for about 1½ hours or until the meat is tender.

Blend the flour to a smooth paste with a small quantity of cold water in a saucepan. Strain the liquid from the meat, measure off 250ml/½ pint liquid, and gradually stir it into the blended flour. Bring to the boil, stirring all the time, and boil for 2–3 minutes. Add this sauce to the meat and re-heat if necessary. Spoon or pipe the hot creamed potatoes in a border on a warmed serving dish and arrange the meat in the centre. Sprinkle the chopped capers over the meat.

HARICOT OF LAMB OR MUTTON

6 helpings

1kg/2lb middle neck of lamb *or*
   scrag end of mutton
25g/1oz butter *or* dripping
1 large onion
2 cloves garlic

25g/1oz plain flour
800ml/1 pint 12fl oz chicken stock
bouquet garni
salt and pepper

GARNISH

2 carrots

1 turnip

Wipe the meat and trim off any skin and excess fat. Cut the meat into serving-sized pieces or cutlets. Melt the fat in a large saucepan and fry the meat quickly until sealed and lightly browned. Skin and chop the onion, and skin and crush the garlic. Fry them in the fat until softened but not coloured. Stir in the flour and cook gently until browned. Draw the pan off the heat and gradually add the stock. Return to the heat and stir until boiling. Add the bouquet garni, seasoning, and meat. Cover with a lid and simmer over gentle heat for about 2 hours until the meat is tender.

Meanwhile, prepare the carrots and turnip for the garnish and cut them into 6mm/¼ inch dice. Add the vegetable trimmings to the meat whilst it is cooking. Cook the diced vegetables separately from the meat in boiling salted water until just tender.

When cooked, arrange the meat on a warmed serving dish. If necessary, boil the stock in the saucepan rapidly to reduce it, then strain it over the meat. Garnish the meat with the cooked diced vegetables.

LAMB CUTLETS IN ASPIC

8 helpings

8 cutlets from best end of leg of lamb
salt and pepper

750ml/1½ pints aspic jelly

GARNISH

100g/4oz cooked green peas
100g/4oz cooked sliced green beans

2×15ml spoons/2 tablespoons mayonnaise *or* French dressing
½ lettuce

Wipe and trim the cutlets neatly. Season with salt and pepper. Either grill, shallow fry or braise the cutlets. Although grilling and frying are simpler and quicker methods, braising is recommended because it imparts extra flavour. When cooked, leave the cutlets until cold, covered with a light cloth.

Melt the aspic jelly and pour a thin layer of it into a large dish rinsed with cold water. Leave to set. Cool the remaining jelly until cold but not set. Brush the cutlets with the cold, liquid aspic and lay them about 1.25cm/½ inch apart on the jelly, with each bone curving the same way. Pour the remaining jelly gently over the cutlets and leave to set. Then turn out on to a sheet of greaseproof paper laid on a chilled metal tray.

Mix the cooked peas and beans with the mayonnaise or French dressing and spoon them into the centre of a round dish. With a sharp knife dipped in hot water, cut out the cutlets and arrange them in a circle around the dish, with the bones pointing inwards. Shred the lettuce and arrange it outside the circle of cutlets. Chop the aspic remaining in the dish and use to garnish the cutlets.

Lamb Cutlets in Aspic

IRISH STEW

4–6 helpings

1kg/2lb middle neck *or* scrag end of neck of lamb *or* mutton	1kg/2lb potatoes
	salt and pepper
2 large onions	water as required

GARNISH

2×15ml spoons/2 tablespoons
   chopped parsley

Wipe the meat, cut it into neat cutlets or pieces, and trim off any excess fat. Skin the onions and slice them thinly; prepare and slice the potatoes. In a stewpan, place the layers of meat, onions, and potatoes, adding seasoning between each layer, and finishing with a layer of potatoes. Add enough water to come half-way up the meat and vegetables. Cover the pan with a lid, heat to simmering point, and simmer gently for 2½ hours. Alternatively, cook the stew in a casserole, covered with a lid, in a fairly hot oven, 190°C/375°F/Gas 5, for 2–2½ hours. Serve garnished with chopped parsley.

Irish Stew

MOUSSAKA

4 helpings

1 medium-sized aubergine
salt
1 large onion
1 clove of garlic
2 medium-sized tomatoes
2×15ml spoons/2 tablespoons olive oil
500g/1lb raw lamb, minced
pepper

1×10ml spoon/1 dessertspoon parsley
150ml/6fl oz dry white wine
300ml/12fl oz milk
1 egg
2 egg yolks
a pinch of grated nutmeg
75g/3oz Kefalotiri *or* Parmesan cheese
fat for greasing

Cut the aubergine into 1.25cm/½ inch slices, sprinkle them with salt and put to one side on a large platter to drain. Chop the onion, grate the garlic, and skin, de-seed, and chop the tomatoes. Heat the olive oil, add the onion and garlic, and sauté gently until the onion is soft. Add the minced meat, and continue cooking, stirring with a fork to break up any lumps in the meat. When the meat is thoroughly browned, add salt, pepper, parsley, and the tomatoes. Mix well, and add the white wine. Simmer the mixture for a few minutes to blend the flavours, then remove from the heat.

In a basin, beat together the milk, egg, egg yolks, salt, and a good pinch of grated nutmeg. Grate the cheese, add about half to the egg mixture, and beat again briefly.

Grease a 20×10×10cm/8×4×4 inch oven-to-table baking dish. Drain the aubergine slices and pat dry with soft kitchen paper. Place half in the bottom of the casserole and cover with the meat mixture. Lay the remaining aubergine slices on the meat and pour the milk and egg mixture over them. Sprinkle the remaining cheese on top. Bake in a moderate oven, 180°C/350°F/Gas 4, for 30–40 minutes, until the custard is set and the top is light golden-brown. Serve from the dish.

Note Moussaka can be made a day ahead, then re-heated, covered in a warm oven.

Moussaka

BLANQUETTE OF LAMB

5–6 helpings

1kg/2lb lean best end of neck *or* middle neck *or* breast of lamb
salt and pepper
water to cover
1 large onion
bouquet garni
6 black peppercorns
a pinch of grated nutmeg

2 × 15ml spoons/2 tablespoons butter *or* margarine
2 × 15ml spoons/2 tablespoons plain flour
1 egg yolk
2 × 15ml spoons/2 tablespoons single cream *or* milk

GARNISH
100g/4oz baked button mushrooms

Wipe the meat. Bone it and cut into pieces about 5cm/2 inches square. Put the meat into a stewpan with the salt and water to cover. Heat to boiling point. Skin and slice the onion and add it to the pan with the bouquet garni, peppercorns, and nutmeg. Reduce the heat, cover the pan with a tight-fitting lid, and simmer for 1½–2 hours until the meat is tender. When cooked, transfer the meat to a warmed serving dish, cover, and keep hot. Strain the liquid from the meat and measure off 250ml/½ pint.

Melt the butter or margarine in a saucepan, stir in the flour, and cook gently for 2–3 minutes without browning it. Gradually add the stock and stir until boiling, then reduce the heat and simmer for 3 minutes. Beat together the egg yolk and the cream or milk. Stir a little of the hot sauce into the egg yolk mixture, then add the mixture to the rest of the sauce off the heat. Return to the heat, stir, and cook very gently until the egg yolk thickens the sauce, but do not allow the sauce to boil or it may curdle. Season to taste. Strain the sauce over the meat. Garnish with the button mushrooms.

LAMB OR MUTTON ROLL

6 helpings

650g/1lb 5oz lean ham *or* mutton
200g/7oz ham *or* bacon
1 × 2.5ml spoon/½ teaspoon finely chopped onion
3 × 15ml spoons/3 tablespoons soft white breadcrumbs
1 × 5ml spoon/1 teaspoon chopped parsley
½ × 2.5ml spoon/¼ teaspoon dried mixed herbs
a pinch of grated nutmeg

1 × 2.5ml spoon/½ teaspoon grated lemon rind
salt and pepper
1 egg
2 × 15ml spoons/2 tablespoons chicken stock
1 × 15ml spoon/1 tablespoon plain flour *or* beaten egg and 2 × 15ml spoons/2 tablespoons breadcrumbs
2 × 15ml spoons/2 tablespoons dripping

Wipe the lamb or mutton. Finely chop or mince all the meat. Put in a bowl and mix it well with the onion, breadcrumbs, herbs, nutmeg, and grated lemon rind. Season to taste. Beat the egg until liquid, and add it with the stock to moisten the mixture. Shape it into a short thick roll. Wrap the roll in foil or several thicknesses of greaseproof paper to keep it in shape and to protect the meat. Bake in a moderate oven, 180°C/350°F/Gas 4, for 1½ hours.

Remove the foil or paper and lightly dredge the roll with the flour, or brush it with the beaten egg and coat it with breadcrumbs. Heat the dripping in a baking tin and place the roll in the tin. Baste well and return it to the oven for a further 30 minutes until browned.

Serve with gravy.

Note Under-cooked cold lamb or mutton can be used. The roll should then be cooked for only 1 hour before browning it.

DEVILLED KIDNEYS

4 helpings

4 sheep's *or* 8 lamb's kidneys
3 × 10ml spoons/3 dessertspoons
   dripping *or* oil
1 × 15ml spoon/1 tablespoon
   chopped onion
1 × 2.5ml spoon/½ teaspoon salt
½ × 2.5ml spoon/¼ teaspoon
   Cayenne pepper
1 × 15ml spoon/1 tablespoon
   chutney

2 × 5ml spoons/2 teaspoons lemon
   juice
1 × 2.5ml spoon/½ teaspoon
   prepared mustard
125ml/¼ pint beef stock
2 egg yolks
soft white breadcrumbs

Skin, core, and cut the kidneys in half lengthways, then cut them into neat pieces. Heat the dripping or oil in a small pan, add the onion, and cook gently until softened but not browned. Add the kidney, salt, Cayenne pepper, chutney, lemon juice, mustard, and stock. Heat to boiling point, reduce the heat, cover the pan, and simmer gently for 15–20 minutes, until the kidney is cooked. Cool slightly. Beat the egg yolks lightly and stir them in. Sprinkle in enough breadcrumbs to make the mixture a soft consistency. Re-season if required.

Serve on buttered toast or in a border of hot creamed potatoes.

KIDNEYS.

LIVER HOT POT

6 helpings

500g/1lb sheep's *or* lamb's liver
3 × 15ml spoons/3 tablespoons
   plain flour
salt and pepper
800g/1lb 10oz potatoes
2 large onions

fat for greasing
500ml/1 pint beef stock
6 rashers streaky bacon, without
   rinds

Remove the skin and tubes from the liver. Season the flour with salt and pepper. Dip each slice of liver in the seasoned flour. Prepare the potatoes and onions and slice them thinly. Arrange layers of liver, onion, and potatoes in a greased casserole, ending with a neat layer of potatoes. Heat the stock and pour in just enough to cover the potatoes. Cover the casserole with a lid. Bake in a moderate oven, 180°C/350°F/Gas 4, for about 1 hour or until the liver is tender.

Remove the lid and arrange the bacon rashers on top. Continue cooking without a lid until the bacon is crisp. Serve from the casserole.

VEAL

STUFFED BREAST OF VEAL

a thick end of breast of veal
  (1kg/2lb approx)
salt and pepper
300g/10oz pork sausage-meat
1 large onion
1 large carrot
½ turnip

bouquet garni
6 black peppercorns
water to cover
butter for greasing
250g/8oz short-grain rice
50g/2oz grated Parmesan cheese

GARNISH

slices of lemon

Remove all bones and tendons from the meat. Wipe, then season well. Spread the sausage-meat evenly over the inner surface of the meat, roll up and tie securely with fine string. Prepare and slice the vegetables. Put them with the bones and trimmings in a large pan. Add the bouquet garni, peppercorns, salt and pepper, and enough water to cover the vegetables. Place the meat on top, cover with buttered greaseproof paper and a tight-fitting lid. Heat to boiling point, reduce the heat and simmer gently for about 2½ hours. Baste occasionally and add more water if necessary. Transfer the meat to a warmed dish and keep hot.

Strain off the liquid and make it up to 750ml/1½ pints with water. Put the stock in a pan and bring to the boil. Wash the rice and cook it in the stock until the stock is absorbed. Season to taste and stir in the cheese. Place the rice in a layer on a warmed serving dish and put the meat on top. Garnish with slices of lemon.

ESCALOPES OF VEAL
(Wiener Schnitzel)

6 thin escalopes of veal
  (12.5×7.5cm/5×3 inches
  approx)
plain flour
salt and pepper
1 egg

2–3 drops oil
dried white breadcrumbs for
  coating
butter *or* oil and butter for frying

GARNISH

6 crimped lemon slices

1×15ml spoon/1 tablespoon
  chopped parsley

Wipe the meat. Season the flour with salt and pepper. Dip the escalopes in the seasoned flour. Beat the egg until liquid with the oil. Brush the escalopes with the egg mixture and coat with breadcrumbs, pressing them on well. Heat the butter or mixture of oil and butter in a large frying pan. Put in the escalopes and fry over moderate to gentle heat for 7–10 minutes, turning them once only.

Remove the escalopes and place them, overlapping slightly, on a warmed, flat serving dish. Garnish the middle of each escalope with a crimped slice of lemon sprinkled with parsley.

BARDED ROAST BEST END NECK OF VEAL

4 helpings

a best end of neck of veal (1kg/2lb approx)
larding bacon
2 medium-sized carrots
1 medium-sized onion
1 small turnip
2 sticks celery
salt
bouquet garni
10 white peppercorns
125–250ml/¼–½ pint chicken stock
butter for greasing
fat *or* oil for basting
25g/1oz butter *or* margarine
25g/1oz plain flour

Wipe the meat. Fold the flap of meat under the joint. Bard the upper surface (flesh side) in close rows with thin 3.75cm/1½ inch strips of fat bacon. Prepare and slice the carrots, onion, turnip and celery. Put the vegetables in a large pan with the salt, bouquet garni, peppercorns, and just enough stock to cover them. Lay the meat on top, cover with buttered greaseproof paper and a tight-fitting lid, and cook gently for 2 hours. Add more stock, if needed.

When cooked, remove the meat from the pan. Heat some fat or oil in a roasting tin. Put the meat into the hot fat or oil, baste well and bake in a moderate oven, 180°C/350°F/Gas 4, for 30 minutes, basting after 15 minutes. Transfer the meat to a warmed dish and keep hot. Strain and measure the stock in which the meat was cooked and make up to 375ml/¾ pint with water.

Heat the butter or margarine in a pan. Stir in the flour and cook gently until browned. Gradually add the stock to the roux and stir until boiling. Reduce the heat and simmer for 5 minutes. Season to taste. Serve the sauce separately.

Suffed Breast of Veal

VITELLO TONNATA

(Cold Veal with Tuna Sauce)

6–8 helpings

5 anchovy fillets	1 medium-sized carrot
1kg/2lb leg of veal, boned	2 sticks celery
salt and pepper	375ml/¾ pint dry white wine
pared rind and juice of 1 lemon	100g/4oz canned tuna fish in oil
1 onion	100ml/4fl oz olive oil *or* as needed
2 cloves	1×15ml spoon/1 tablespoon capers
2 bay leaves	

GARNISH

lemon slices

Drain the anchovy fillets. Remove the thin outer skin and any solid fat from the veal. Place 3 anchovy fillets along the length of the cavity where the bone was removed. Reshape the meat and tie it into a neat roll about 20×15cm/8×6 inches. Season the meat. Put it in a stewpan with a strip of lemon rind. Skin the onion, press in the cloves, and add it to the pan with the bay leaves. Slice and add the carrot and celery. Pour in the wine, and add just enough water to cover the meat. Bring to the boil, cover, reduce the heat, and simmer gently for 1½ hours or until the meat is tender. Remove it from the pan and leave to cool completely. (Keep the stock for another dish.)

When the meat is cold, slice it thinly, then reshape it into the roll. Place it in a deep terrine or serving dish.

Pound the tuna fish with its oil, the lemon juice, and remaining anchovy fillets until smooth. Alternatively, process in an electric blender. When smooth, trickle in the olive oil gradually, as when making mayonnaise, whisking or blending as fast as possible until the mixture thickens. Season to taste. Chop and fold in the capers. Pour the sauce over the meat, cover loosely, and leave to marinate for 12–14 hours. Serve garnished with thin lemon slices.

BRAINS IN BLACK BUTTER

(Cervelles au Beurre Noir)

4 helpings

2 sets calf's brains	bouquet garni
salt	flour for dusting
1×5ml spoon/1 teaspoon lemon juice	ground pepper
1 small onion	2×15ml spoons/2 tablespoons butter
1 litre/2 pints water	butter for greasing
2×15ml spoons/2 tablespoons white wine vinegar	

BLACK BUTTER

4×15ml spoons/4 tablespoons butter	2×15ml spoons/2 tablespoons capers (optional)
1×15ml spoon/1 tablespoon white wine vinegar	

GARNISH

sprig of parsley

Soak the brains for 30 minutes in lightly salted cold water sharpened with the lemon juice to remove all traces of blood. Meanwhile, skin and halve the onion, and put it in a saucepan with the water, vinegar, and bouquet garni. Heat to simmering point and simmer for 30 minutes. Leave the stock to cool.

Drain the brains, and cut off any membranes. Wash thoroughly but very gently. Put the brains into the stock, heat slowly to simmering point, and poach for 20 minutes. Drain thoroughly, and put into very cold water to cool. Drain again and pat dry. Season the flour with salt and pepper, and dust the brains with it. Heat the 2×15ml spoons/2 tablespoons butter in a frying pan, and fry the brains lightly, turning them over, until just browned on all sides. Put them in a shallow serving dish, and keep them warm under buttered paper.

Take any bits of brains out of the frying pan, add the butter for the Black Butter and heat until golden-brown. Add the vinegar, and let it boil up. As soon as it foams, pour the mixture over the brains, adding the capers, if used. Serve at once, garnished with a sprig of parsley.

HUNGARIAN CALF'S LIVER

6 helpings

625g/1¼lb calf's liver
plain flour
salt
paprika

50g/2oz butter
2×15ml spoons/2 tablespoons
finely grated onion
100ml/4 fl oz fresh *or* soured cream

Remove the skin and tubes, and cut the liver into 1.25cm/½ inch slices. Season some flour with salt and paprika. Dip the slices of liver in the flour, then shake off the excess. Heat the butter in a frying pan and fry the liver quickly on both sides until browned, then more slowly until tender. Fry the onion with the liver for about 5 minutes. Remove the liver, arrange the slices down the centre of a warmed serving dish, and keep hot. Pour any excess fat out of the pan, add the cream, and heat gently without boiling. Season to taste. Pour this sauce over the liver. Sprinkle with paprika, and serve very hot.

Vitello Tonnata

Overleaf, from the left:
Ham Slices with Fruit (page 154),
Lamb Shashlik (page 141) and
Escalopes of Veal (page 149)

PORK, BACON & HAM

MRS BEETON'S ROAST GRISKIN OF PORK

4 helpings

1kg/2lb neck end of chine of pork
   or griskin (see **Note**)
flour for dredging
50g/2oz lard
fat for greasing

1×15ml spoon/1 tablespoon dried
   sage
2×10ml spoons/2 dessertspoons
   flour
250ml/½ pint water
salt and pepper

Wipe the meat and dredge it lightly with flour. Melt the lard in a roasting tin and brush some of it over the meat. Put the meat in the tin and roast it in a hot oven, 220°C/425°F/Gas 7, for 10 minutes. Baste well and cover the meat loosely with greased greaseproof paper. Reduce the heat to moderate, 180°C/350°F/Gas 4, and continue to roast the meat for a further 1¾ hours, basting it often. Ten minutes before the end of the cooking time, take out the meat, sprinkle it with sage, and return to the oven, uncovered, to complete the cooking.

When cooked, transfer the meat to a warmed serving dish and keep hot. Pour off all but 1×15ml spoon/1 tablespoon fat in the roasting tin and retain the sediment. Stir in the flour and cook gently over low heat for 3–4 minutes until the flour is lightly browned. Gradually add the water and stir until the gravy thickens slightly. Taste and season with salt and pepper. Simmer for about 1 minute, then strain the gravy into a warmed sauce-boat.

Serve with apple sauce.

Note The griskin is the backbone, spine or chine of a pig cut away when preparing a side for bacon; or it can be a shoulder of pork stripped of fat. As it is sold without rind or fat, it needs frequent basting.

ROAST, BONED, STUFFED PORK

6 helpings

1.5kg/3lb boned bladebone
   of pork

3×15ml spoons/3 tablespoons oil

STUFFING

1 medium-sized onion
1 stick of celery
100g/4oz flat mushrooms
25g/1oz butter *or* margarine
50g/2oz canned *or* frozen
   sweetcorn
50g/2oz white breadcrumbs

1×15ml spoon/1 tablespoon
   chopped parsley
salt and pepper
1×2.5ml spoon/½ teaspoon
   ground mace
1×5ml spoon/1 teaspoon lemon
   juice

Wipe the meat and deeply score the rind of the meat if not done by the butcher.

Make the stuffing. Prepare the onion, celery and mushrooms, and chop them finely. Melt the butter or margarine in a small pan and fry the onion and celery until lightly browned. Remove from the heat. Add the mushrooms, sweetcorn, breadcrumbs and parsley, and mix well. Season to taste, and add the mace and lemon juice.

Spoon the stuffing evenly into the 'pocket' left after the meat was boned. Roll up the joint and tie with thin string at regular intervals. Heat 2×15ml spoons/2 tablespoons oil in a roasing tin, then put in the joint. Brush the rind with the remaining oil and sprinkle generously with salt. Roast in a fairly hot oven, 200°C/400°F/Gas 6, for 20–30 minutes, until the crackling is browned. Reduce the heat to moderate, 180°C/350°F/Gas 4, and continue to cook for 1½ hours or until the internal temperature reaches 85–88°C/185–190°F on a meat thermometer. Transfer the joint to a warmed serving dish, remove the string, and keep the meat hot. Pour off the fat in the roasting tin, then prepare a gravy using the sediment left in the tin.

HAM SLICES WITH FRUIT

3 main-course or 6 light first-course or supper helpings

6 ham *or* gammon slices *or* steaks
  (1.25cm/½ inch thick approx)
150g/5oz soft light brown sugar

75g/3oz soft white breadcrumbs
200ml/8floz pineapple juice

GARNISH
2 apples

75g/3oz margarine

Remove the rind from the ham or gammon and snip the fat at intervals to prevent curling. Put the slices or steaks in a frying pan with a very little water, heat to simmering point, and simmer for 10 minutes, turning them once. Drain. Lay the slices or steaks in an overlapping layer in a large, shallow, ovenproof baking dish. Mix together the sugar and breadcrumbs, and spread it over the slices or steaks, then trickle the pineapple juice over them. Bake uncovered, in a moderate oven, 180°C/350°F/Gas 4, for 25 minutes.

Meanwhile, peel, core, and cut the apples into rings, 2.5cm/1 inch thick (approx). Melt the margarine in a frying pan, and fry the rings until tender but not soft. Decorate the cooked dish with the apple rings, and serve at once.

PORK SAUSAGES WITH CABBAGE

4 helpings

1 hard white cabbage
  (1kg/2lb approx)
1 small onion
75g/3oz butter

salt and pepper
125ml/¼ pint water
500g/1lb pork sausages
  (50g/2oz each)

Trim the cabbage, and cut it into quarters. Shred it finely lengthways. Skin and chop the onion finely. Melt the butter in a large saucepan, and fry the onion in it until transparent. Add the cabbage, salt and pepper, and water. Cover the pan with a tight-fitting lid and cook over gentle heat for 1 hour.

Meanwhile, fry, bake or grill the sausages until cooked through. Drain any liquid from the cooked cabbage and pile the vegetable on a warmed serving dish. Arrange the hot sausages on or around the cabbage.

FRIED SAUSAGES.

HAM WITH RAISIN SAUCE

8–10 helpings

1.5–2kg/3–4lb parboiled York
  ham
250g/8oz dark soft brown sugar

cloves
100ml/4fl oz white wine vinegar

RAISIN SAUCE

50g/2oz soft dark brown sugar
1×2.5ml spoon/½ teaspoon
  English mustard
1×15ml spoon/1 tablespoon
  cornflour

75g/3oz seedless raisins
1×15ml spoon/1 tablespoon grated
  orange rind
100ml/4fl oz fresh orange juice
200ml/8fl oz water

Put the ham in a shallow baking tin and bake, uncovered, in a warm oven, 160°C/325°F/Gas 3, for 10 minutes per 500g/1lb meat. Thirty minutes before the end of the cooking time, lift out the meat and remove the rind. Score the fat in a pattern of diamonds. Cover the fat with brown sugar and press in cloves at the points of the diamond pattern. Trickle the wine vinegar gently over the ham. Continue baking, basting with the juices, until the ham is fully cooked.

Make the Raisin Sauce. Mix together in a saucepan the brown sugar, mustard and cornflour. Add the rest of the ingredients and cook very gently for 10 minutes or until syrupy.

Transfer the cooked ham to a warmed serving dish and serve the sauce separately in a sauce-boat.

Ham with Raisin Sauce

GAMMON STEAKS WITH MARMALADE

4 helpings

4 medium-sized gammon steaks
ground pepper
1 small onion
1×5ml spoon/1 teaspoon butter *or* margarine

4×15ml spoons/4 tablespoons medium-cut orange marmalade
2×5ml spoons/2 teaspoons vinegar

GARNISH

chopped parsley

Remove the rind from the gammon steaks and snip the fat at intervals to prevent curling. Place on a grill rack and season with pepper to taste. Cook under a moderate grill, turning once, for 10–15 minutes depending on the thickness of the steaks. When cooked, transfer the steaks to a warmed serving dish and keep hot.

Skin the onion and chop it finely. Melt the fat in a pan and cook the onion gently for 5 minutes without browning it. Draw the pan off the heat and stir in the marmalade and vinegar, with any fat and juices left in the grill pan. Return to the heat and heat to boiling point, to reduce slightly.

Spoon the sauce over the gammon steaks. Garnish with chopped parsley and serve at once.

THE NUTMEG.

GRILLED CRUMBED PORK CHOPS OR CUTLETS

6 helpings

6 pork chops *or* cutlets
1 egg
1×5ml spoon/1 teaspoon dried sage

salt and pepper
soft white breadcrumbs
3×15ml spoons/3 tablespoons oil

Wipe the chops or cutlets and trim off any excess fat. Beat the egg until liquid and mix with the sage, salt and pepper. Brush the chops or cutlets on both sides with the beaten egg, then coat them carefully with the breadcrumbs. Brush carefully with some oil, then brush the grill rack with the remaining oil. Cook under a moderate grill for about 20 minutes, turning often, until golden-brown and cooked through.

MRS BEETON'S OXFORD SAUSAGES

Makes 36 sausages or 60–70 chipolatas

1.5kg/3lb pork or 0.5kg/1lb lean
  pork, 0.5kg/1lb lean veal and
  0.5kg/1lb beef dripping
500g/1lb soft white breadcrumbs
1×5ml spoon/1 teaspoon ground
  pepper

grated rind of ½ lemon
grated nutmeg
6 chopped sage leaves
1×2.5ml spoon/½ teaspoon
  chopped winter savory
1×2.5ml spoon/½ teaspoon
  marjoram

Choose pork which consists of two-thirds lean meat to one third
fat, without skin and gristle. Cut it up roughly and mince it finely
or coarsely, according to taste; for a fine cut, however, it must be
put through the coarse plate first, otherwise it will clog the
machine. Mix the rest of the ingredients into the sausage-meat and
mince again. Fill the sausage-meat into skins using a
sausage-filler, or make it into little cakes or cork shapes. Allow to
mature for 12–14 hours in a cool place, to develop flavour and
texture.

Gammon Steaks with Marmalade

PORK AND APPLE HOT POT

4 loin *or* spare rib chops
1 medium-sized cooking apple
1 medium-sized onion
50g/2oz lard *or* oil
100g/4oz mushrooms

fat for greasing
1 × 2.5ml spoon/½ teaspoon dried
    sage *or* savory
500g/1lb potatoes
salt and pepper

GARNISH

chopped parsley

Wipe the chops and trim off any excess fat. Prepare the apple and onion and slice them thinly. Heat the lard or oil in a pan and fry the apple and onion until golden-brown. Clean and slice the mushrooms.

Grease a casserole and put the mushrooms in the bottom. Lay the chops on the mushrooms and cover with the apple and onion. Sprinkle the herb over the top. Prepare the potatoes and cut them into 1.25cm/½ inch cubes. Top the casserole with the potatoes and brush them with the fat remaining in the pan. Season with salt and pepper. Pour in enough water to come half-way up the meat and vegetables. Cover the pan with a tight-fitting lid and cook in a moderate oven, 180°C/350°F/Gas 4, for 1½ hours. Remove the lid 30 minutes before the end of the cooking time to allow the potatoes to brown. Garnish with chopped parsley and serve from the casserole.

FAGGOTS OR SAVOURY DUCKS

800g/1lb 10oz pig's liver
100g/4oz fat belly of pork
2 medium-sized onions
a pinch of dried thyme
1 × 2.5ml spoon/½ teaspoon dried
    sage
a pinch of dried basil (optional)

salt and pepper
a pinch of grated nutmeg
1 egg
100g/4oz soft white breadcrumbs
caul fat *or* flour, as preferred
fat for greasing

Remove the skin and tubes of the liver, then slice it. Slice the pork belly. Skin and slice the onions. Put the meat and onions in a saucepan with just enough water to cover them. Heat to boiling point, cover the pan, reduce the heat, and simmer for 30 minutes. Strain off the liquid and reserve it for the gravy.

Mince the meat and onions finely. Add the herbs, salt, pepper, and nutmeg. Beat the egg until liquid and stir it in. Mix in enough breadcrumbs to make a mixture which can be moulded. Divide it into 8 equal portions and shape them into round balls. Cut squares of caul fat, if used, large enough to encase the balls and wrap each ball in a piece of fat. Alternatively, roll each ball in flour. Lay the faggots side by side in a greased baking tin. Cover the tin loosely with foil. Bake in a moderate oven, 180°C/350°F/Gas 4, for 25 minutes. Remove the foil and bake for 10 minutes to brown the tops of the faggots.

Serve hot, with a thickened gravy made from the cooking liquid.

BRAISED PORK CHOPS IN CIDER

4 helpings

4 middle loin *or* fore loin pork
  chops
4×15ml spoons/4 tablespoons dry
  cider
bouquet garni
2 medium-sized onions
2 cooking apples
a pinch of ground cinnamon

salt and pepper
100g/4oz flat mushrooms
200g/7oz shelled fresh peas
200g/7oz canned whole small
  beetroots
150–200g/5–7oz noodles

Wipe the chops and trim off the rind and excess fat. Heat the rind and fat trimmings in a frying pan until the fat runs. Add the chops and fry, turning once, until golden-brown on both sides. Remove the chops and place them in a casserole. Pour off the excess fat in the frying pan and reserve the rest. Pour the cider over the chops and add the bouquet garni. Cover the casserole and cook over gentle heat or in a warm oven, 160°C/325°F/Gas 3.

Meanwhile, prepare and chop the onions and apples. Put them into the frying pan and fry gently for 5 minutes. Add the cinnamon and just enough water to cover the onions and apples. Cover the pan, heat to simmering point, and simmer for about 15 minutes, until soft. Rub through a sieve, season to taste, and spoon the apple and onion mixture over the chops in the casserole. Replace the lid and cook for 1¾–2 hours in all.

Clean the mushrooms and slice thickly; add them and the peas for the last 30 minutes of the cooking time. Heat the beetroot separately. Cook the noodles in boiling salted water until, when tested, the centre is still slightly firm. Drain the noodles and beetroot. Serve the noodles on a warmed serving dish with the chops on top, and arrange the mushrooms, peas, and beetroots round them.

Braised Pork Chops in Cider

PIG'S TROTTERS IN JELLY

3–4 helpings

4 pig's trotters
2 pig's ears
1 × 10ml spoon/1 dessertspoon
   chopped parsley

1 × 2.5ml spoon/½ teaspoon
   chopped fresh sage
salt and pepper

Singe off the hairs. Wash the trotters and ears thoroughly in salted water. Scald the ears. Put the trotters and ears in a large pan with just enough cold water to cover them. Heat to boiling point, cover the pan with a tight-fitting lid, reduce the heat, and simmer gently for about 3 hours until the bones can be removed easily. Lift out the trotters and ears, reserving the liquid in the pan. Cut the meat into neat dice and replace in the liquid. Add the herbs, and season to taste. Simmer gently for 15 minutes. Turn into a mould or basin and leave until cold and set.

SAGE.

HOT PUDDINGS

For dishing a boiled pudding as soon as it comes out of the pot, dip it into a basin of cold water, and the cloth will then not adhere to it. Great expedition is necessary in sending puddings to table, ·as, by standing, they quickly become heavy, batter puddings particularly.

Isabella Beeton 1861

Left: *Tapioca Cream Pudding (page 166)*
and *Pears in Wine (page 187)*
Below: *Roly-Poly Pudding (page 175)*

MILK PUDDINGS

CARAMEL RICE PUDDING

——— *6 helpings* ———

125g/5oz Carolina *or* similar rice
750ml/1½ pints milk
a pinch of salt
75g/3oz lump sugar

75ml/3fl oz water
2 eggs
40g/1½oz caster sugar

Wash the rice, and put it into a saucepan with the milk and salt. Bring to simmering point and simmer for about 1 hour or until the rice is soft and all the milk has been absorbed.

Meanwhile, prepare a thickly folded band of newspaper long enough to encircle a 1 litre/2 pint charlotte mould (it can then be held firmly in one hand when heated). Heat the mould in boiling water or in the oven and wrap the newspaper round it. Prepare the caramel by heating the sugar and water together, stirring until it boils. Remove the spoon and leave it to boil, without stirring, until golden-brown. Immediately, pour the caramel into the warmed charlotte mould; twist and turn it until the sides and base are evenly coated. Leave to harden for a few minutes.

Beat the eggs until liquid and stir them into the cooked rice with the sugar. Turn into the prepared mould, cover with greased greaseproof paper or foil, and steam for 1 hour or until firm. Turn out, if liked. Serve hot or cold.

LEMON RICE

——— *6 helpings* ———

50g/2oz Carolina *or* similar rice
500ml/1 pint milk
a pinch of salt
pared rind and juice of 1 lemon
75g/3oz granulated sugar
2 eggs

butter for greasing
3×15ml spoons/3 tablespoons
    smooth seedless jam
50g/2oz caster sugar
caster sugar for dredging

Wash the rice and put it in a double boiler with the milk, salt, and lemon rind; simmer for about 1 hour or until tender. Remove the rind and stir in the granulated sugar. Cool slightly. Separate the eggs. Stir the yolks and lemon juice into the rice. Pour into a buttered 1 litre/2 pint dish and bake in a warm oven at 160°C/325°F/Gas 3, for 20–25 minutes. Spread the jam on top of the pudding. Whisk the egg whites until stiff, and fold in the caster sugar. Pile on top of the pudding, dredge with a little extra caster sugar, and bake in a very cool oven at 140°C/275°F/Gas 1, for 20–30 minutes until the meringue is set and coloured.

EARS OF RICE.

WINDSOR PUDDING

6 helpings

40g/1½oz Carolina *or* similar rice
375ml/¾ pint milk
1kg/2lb cooking apples

grated *or* pared rind and juice of ½
   lemon (see Method)
50g/2oz caster sugar
3 eggs
butter for greasing

Wash the rice and simmer it in the milk for 45 minutes – 1 hour or until the rice is tender and all the milk has been absorbed. Cool slightly. Peel, core, and chop the apples roughly, and stew in a covered pan until soft. Shake the pan from time to time to prevent them sticking. Rub the apples through a sieve, then add the grated rind and juice of the lemon. Alternatively, process the apples in an electric blender with the pared rind and juice. Stir the cooked rice into the apples with the sugar. Separate the eggs; whisk the whites until fairly stiff and fold them into the mixture. Put the mixture into a buttered 1 litre/2 pint basin, cover with greased greaseproof paper or foil, and steam very gently for 40–45 minutes.

Serve with Pouring Custard (page 17).

Caramel Rice Pudding

HOT TIMBALE OF SEMOLINA

6 helpings

butter for greasing
500ml/1 pint milk
75g/3oz semolina
50g/2oz caster sugar

a few drops vanilla essence
2 eggs
2×15ml spoons/2 tablespoons
  single cream

DECORATION

6 canned apricot halves
250ml/½ pint apricot syrup from
  can
1 strip angelica

3 glacé cherries
1×10ml spoon/1 dessertspoon
  chopped almonds

Butter a 750ml/1½ pint timbale mould or 8 small dariole moulds. Heat the milk, sprinkle in the semolina, stirring all the time, and simmer for 10–15 minutes until it is cooked. Cool slightly. Add the sugar and vanilla essence. Separate the eggs, and stir the yolks into the mixture. Beat with an electric or rotary whisk until it is nearly cold. Whisk the egg whites until just stiff, and fold into the mixture with the cream. Three-quarters fill the timbale mould or small moulds with the mixture. Cover with greased greaseproof paper or foil. Steam a large mould for about 45 minutes and small moulds for 30 minutes or until set.

Meanwhile, heat the apricots between 2 plates over simmering water. Boil the apricot syrup until well reduced. When the pudding is cooked and set, turn out on to a hot dish and decorate with halved apricots, angelica, glacé cherries and chopped almonds. Pour the syrup round and serve.

Hot Timbale of Semolina

SOURED MILK PANCAKES

4 helpings

100g/4oz plain flour
a pinch of salt
1 egg
125ml/¼ pint soured milk
1×10ml spoon/1 dessertspoon
melted butter

½×2.5ml spoon/¼ teaspoon
bicarbonate of soda
1×10ml spoon/1 dessertspoon hot
water
fat *or* oil for frying
caster sugar

FILLING

250ml/½ pint mashed sweetened
ripe fruit (see **Note**)

Sift the flour and salt into a bowl, make a well in the centre, and add the egg. Stir in the milk, gradually working the flour down from the sides. Beat vigorously until the mixture is smooth and bubbly. Add the butter. Dissolve the bicarbonate of soda in the hot water and stir into the mixture. Pour the batter into a jug. Heat a little fat or oil in a frying pan, and pour off any excess. Pour a little batter into the pan to make a pancake about 7.5cm/3 inches in diameter. As soon as it rises and is brown underneath, but before the bubbles break, turn the pancake over and fry the other side until golden-brown. Keep each cooked pancake warm in a tea-towel. Cook the rest of the batter in the same way, greasing the pan when necessary. The cooked pancakes will be thick and fluffy.

For each person, sandwich 3 pancakes together with the fruit. Sprinkle with caster sugar.

Note Use any soft fruit except currants, eg skinned, stoned peaches, apricots or plums, or well-drained stewed fruit or crushed pineapple.

Soured Milk Pancakes

HONEY PUDDING

125ml/¼ pint milk
25g/1oz semolina
2 eggs
25g/1oz butter
100g/4oz honey

grated rind of ½ lemon
1×2.5ml spoon/½ teaspoon
  ground ginger
150g/5oz stale white breadcrumbs
fat for greasing

Heat the milk, sprinkle in the semolina, and cook for 10 minutes, stirring all the time. Separate the eggs. Add the yolks to the semolina with the butter, honey, lemon rind, ground ginger, and breadcrumbs. Beat well. Whisk the egg whites until fairly stiff and fold into the mixture. Put into a greased 625–750ml/1¼–1½ pint basin, cover with greased greaseproof paper or foil, and steam gently for 1¾–2 hours.

TAPIOCA CREAM PUDDING

75g/3oz tapioca
750ml/1½ pints milk
a pinch of salt
15g/½oz butter or margarine
1×15ml spoon/1 tablespoon caster
  sugar

½×2.5ml spoon/¼ teaspoon
  almond essence
3 eggs
butter for greasing
75g/3oz ratafias or small macaroons

Wash the tapioca and soak in the milk for 1–2 hours with the salt. Heat to simmering point, and simmer for about 1 hour until the grain is soft and all the milk has been absorbed. Add the butter, sugar, and essence. Cool slightly. Separate the eggs and stir the yolks into the tapioca. Pour the mixture into a buttered 1 litre/2 pint pie dish, and bake in a moderate oven at 180°C/350°F/Gas 4, for 15–20 minutes. Crush the ratafias or macaroons. Whisk the egg whites until stiff and fold in the biscuits. Pile on top of the tapioca. Bake in a very cool oven at 140°C/275°F/Gas 1, for 20–30 minutes.

MACAROONS.

HONESTY PUDDING

50g/2oz fine oatmeal
1×15ml spoon/1 tablespoon plain
   flour
750ml/1½ pints milk
1 egg

a pinch of salt
1×2.5ml spoon/¼ teaspoon grated
   orange rind
fat for greasing

Blend the oatmeal and flour to a smooth paste in a basin with a little of the milk. Bring the rest of the milk to the boil, and pour it over the mixture, stirring all the time. Return the mixture to the pan and cook over low heat for 5 minutes, stirring all the time. Remove from the heat, and cool for 5 minutes. Beat the egg until liquid, and then beat it into the cooled oatmeal mixture, Flavour with the salt and orange rind. Pour the mixture into a greased 750ml/1½ pint pie dish and bake in a moderate oven, 180°C/350°F/Gas 4, for 35–40 minutes.

Serve hot from the dish, with cream and brown sugar.

CUSTARD PUDDINGS

CUP OR 'BOILED' CUSTARD

(Coating Custard)

4 helpings or 500ml/1 pint (approx)

500ml/1 pint milk
4 eggs *or* 3 eggs and 2 yolks

25g/1oz caster sugar
flavouring

Warm the milk to approximately 65°C/149°F. Mix the eggs and sugar together well, and stir in the milk. Strain the custard into a saucepan or into a heat-proof bowl placed over a pan of simmering water. Alternatively, use a double boiler, but make sure the water does not touch the upper pan. Cook over very gentle heat for 15–25 minutes, stirring all the time with a wooden spoon, until the custard thickens to the consistency of single cream. Stir well round the sides as well as the base of the pan or basin to prevent lumps forming, especially if using a double boiler. Do *not* let the custard boil. If it shows the slightest sign of curdling, put the pan or bowl into a bowl of cold water, or turn the custard into a clean basin and whisk rapidly.

As soon as the custard thickens, pour it into a jug to stop further cooking. Keep it warm by standing the jug in a basin of hot water. If it is to be served cold, pour into a basin and cover with a piece of dampened greaseproof paper to prevent a skin forming. When cold, pour into a serving dish.

VARIATION

POURING CUSTARD

Make as above but use only 3 eggs or 2 eggs and 2 yolks. The custard will thicken only to the consistency of thin single cream or top of the milk.

QUEEN OF PUDDINGS

4 helpings

75g/3oz soft white breadcrumbs
400ml/16fl oz milk
25g/1oz butter
2×5ml spoons/2 teaspoons grated
  lemon rind

2 eggs
75g/3oz caster sugar
fat for greasing
2×15ml spoons/2 tablespoons red
  jam

Dry the breadcrumbs slightly by placing in a cool oven for a few moments. Warm the milk with the butter and lemon rind, to approximately 65°C/149°F; do not let it come near the boil. Separate the eggs and stir 25g/1oz of the sugar into the yolks. Pour the warmed milk over the yolks, and stir in well. Add the crumbs and mix thoroughly. Pour the custard mixture into a greased 750ml/1½ pint pie dish and leave to stand for 30 minutes. Bake in a warm oven at 160°C/325°F/Gas 3, for 40–45 minutes until the pudding is lightly set.

Remove the pudding from the oven and reduce the temperature to 120°C/250°F/Gas ½. Warm the jam and spread it over the pudding. Whisk the egg whites until stiff, add half the remaining sugar and whisk again. Fold in nearly all the remaining sugar. Spoon the meringue round the edge of the jam and sprinkle with the remainder of the caster sugar. (The piled-up meringue and the red jam centre then suggest a crown.) Return the pudding to the oven for 40–45 minutes or until the meringue is set.

Opposite, from the left:
Orange Custard (page 173),
Queen of Puddings (page 169) and
Floating Islands (page 173)

CRÈME BRÛLÉE

4 helpings

1×15ml spoon/1 tablespoon
  cornflour
250ml/½ pint milk
250ml/½ pint cream
a few drops vanilla essence

3 eggs
50g/2oz caster sugar
fat for greasing
ground cinnamon (optional)

Blend the cornflour to a smooth paste with a little of the milk, and bring the rest of the milk to the boil. Pour the boiling milk on to the blended cornflour, stirring well. Return the mixture to the pan, bring to the boil and boil for 1 minute, stirring all the time. Remove from the heat and leave to cool. Beat together the cream, vanilla essence, and eggs. Stir into the cooled mixture. Whisk over low heat for about 30 minutes or until the custard thickens; do not boil. Add 25g/1oz sugar and pour into a greased 625ml/1¼ pint flameproof dish. Sprinkle the pudding with the rest of the sugar and a little cinnamon, if used. Place under a hot grill for 10 minutes or until the sugar has melted and turned brown. Keep the custard about 10cm/4 inches from the heat. Serve hot or cold.

Alternatively, bake in a fairly hot oven at 200°C/400°F/Gas 6, for about 15 minutes until the pudding is browned.

BREAD AND BUTTER PUDDING

4 helpings

butter for greasing
4 thin slices bread (100g/4oz approx)
25g/1oz butter
50g/2oz sultanas *or* currants
a pinch of nutmeg *or* cinnamon
400ml/16fl oz milk
2 eggs
25g/1oz granulated sugar

Grease a 1 litre/2 pint pie dish. Cut the crusts off the bread and spread the slices with the butter. Cut the bread into squares or triangles and arrange in alternate layers, buttered side up, with the sultanas or currants. Sprinkle each layer lightly with spice. Arrange the top layer of bread in an attractive pattern. Warm the milk to approximately 65°C/149°F; do not let it come near the boil. Beat together the eggs and most of the sugar with a fork and stir in the milk. Strain the custard over the bread, sprinkle some nutmeg and the remaining sugar on top, and leave to stand for 30 minutes. Bake in a moderate oven at 180°C/350°F/Gas 4, for 30–40 minutes until set and lightly browned.

WINTER PUDDING

4 helpings

500g/1lb cooking apples
75g/3oz cooking dates
75g/3oz seedless raisins
25g/1oz cut mixed peel
1×5ml spoon/1 teaspoon grated nutmeg
2 pieces plain cake *or* trifle sponges (5×7.5cm/2×3 inches approx)
2 eggs
300ml/12fl oz milk
fat for greasing

Peel, core, and slice the apples. Chop the dates. Put with the raisins, peel, nutmeg, and a little water into a saucepan, cover, and simmer gently until tender. Crumble the cake finely. Beat the eggs lightly with a fork and stir in the milk. Add the crumbs, stir, and leave to stand for 10 minutes. Drain the stewed fruit, put it into a greased 750ml/1½ pint pie dish and level the top. Pour the custard mixture over the fruit. Bake in a warm oven at 160°C/325°F/Gas 3, for 1–1¼ hours until the top of the pudding is browned.

Serve with cream.

THE LEMON.

LEMON DELICIOUS PUDDING

4 helpings

3 eggs
1×15ml spoon/1 tablespoon
  self-raising flour
75g/3oz caster sugar
200ml/8fl oz milk
juice and grated rind of 2 large
  lemons

a pinch of salt
1×15ml spoon/1 tablespoon icing
  sugar
butter for greasing

Separate the eggs, Sift the flour. Beat the yolks with the caster
sugar until light, pale and creamy. Whisk the milk, flour, lemon
juice, and rind into the egg yolks. Whisk the egg whites with the
salt, adding the icing sugar gradually. Continue to whisk until stiff
but not dry. Fold into the lemon mixture. Grease a deep 1 litre/2
pint ovenproof dish and pour the mixture into it. Stand the dish in
a shallow pan of cold water and bake in a moderate oven at
180°C/350°F/Gas 4, for 1 hour.

Note This pudding has a light spongy top with lemon sauce
underneath.

Bread and Butter Pudding

CABINET PUDDING

50g/2oz glacé cherries *or* seedless
   raisins
2×15ml spoons/2 tablespoons
   medium-sweet sherry
fat for greasing
4 individual trifle sponges
   (5×7.5cm/2×3 inches approx)

9 ratafias *or* 2 macaroons
400ml/16fl oz milk
3 eggs
25g/1oz caster sugar
a few drops vanilla essence

DECORATION

glacé cherries

angelica

Soak the glacé cherries or raisins in the sherry. Grease a 12.5cm/5 inch round cake tin and line the base with oiled greaseproof paper. Cut up the cherries and angelica for the decoration. Decorate the bottom of the tin with them. Cut the sponges into 1.25cm/½ inch dice, crumble the ratafias or macaroons and mix them together. Drain the dried fruit. Put alternate layers of cake and fruit in the tin. Warm the milk to approximately 65°C/149°F; do not let it come near the boil. Beat the eggs and sugar together with a fork and stir in the milk. Add a few drops of vanilla essence. Strain the custard into the tin slowly, so as not to disturb the decoration. Leave to stand for 1 hour. Cover with greased foil or greaseproof paper and steam gently for 1 hour. Remove the pudding from the steamer, leave to stand for a few minutes, turn out on to a warmed dish and peel off the paper.

ORANGE CUSTARD

pared rind and juice of 3 oranges
50g/2oz caster sugar

375ml/¾ pint boiling water
4 eggs

Put the orange rind, sugar, and boiling water into a basin, cover and leave for 2 hours. Strain the liquid into a pan, and warm but do not boil it. Beat the eggs together and stir in the liquid. Strain the custard into the pan and heat very gently, stirring all the time with a wooden spoon until the custard thickens. Do not boil or the mixture will curdle. Strain the orange juice into the custard, and stir. Pour into 4 glasses and serve warm or chilled, topped with cream.

BAKED SOUFFLÉ OMELET

fat for greasing
4×15ml spoons/4 tablespoons jam
   or stewed fruit
4 eggs
50g/2oz caster sugar

2×15ml spoons/2 tablespoons
   water
a pinch of salt
caster *or* icing sugar for dredging

Heat the oven to fairly hot, 190°C/375°F/Gas 5. Grease a shallow 22.5cm/9 inch ovenproof dish and spread the jam or fruit over the base. Separate the eggs. Beat the yolks with the sugar and add the water. Whisk the egg whites and salt until stiff and fold into the yolk mixture. Pour over the jam or fruit and bake for 15–20 minutes. Dredge with sugar, and serve at once.

FLOATING ISLANDS

4 helpings

3 eggs
200g/7oz caster sugar

500ml/1 pint milk
a few drops vanilla essence

Separate the eggs. Whisk the egg whites until very stiff. Fold in 150g/5oz caster sugar. Pour the milk into a frying pan and add a few drops of vanilla essence. Heat gently until the surface of the milk is just shivering. It must not boil or the milk will discolour and form a skin. Using 2 dessertspoons, mould egg shapes from the meringue and slide them into the milk. Make only a few at a time, and leave plenty of space between them in the pan as they swell when cooking. Cook slowly for 5 minutes, then turn them over, using a palette knife and a spoon, and cook for a further 5 minutes. They are very delicate and must be handled with care. Remove from the milk gently and place on a cloth or soft kitchen paper to drain. Continue making shapes from the meringue and poaching them in milk, until all the meringue is used. Arrange the 'islands' in a flat serving dish.

Blend the egg yolks with the rest of the sugar, then stir in the milk gently, stirring all the time, until the sauce thickens slightly. Do not let it come near the boil or it will curdle. Pour the custard round the 'islands' and serve at once.

Cabinet Pudding

BOILED & STEAMED PUDDINGS

GOLDEN SYRUP PUDDING

6–7 helpings

fat for greasing
3×15ml spoons/3 tablespoons
    golden syrup
150g/5oz plain flour
1×5ml spoon/1 teaspoon
    bicarbonate of soda
a pinch of salt
1×5ml spoon/1 teaspoon ground
    ginger

150g/5oz stale white breadcrumbs
100g/4oz shredded suet
50g/2oz caster sugar
1 egg
1×15ml spoon/1 tablespoon black
    treacle
75–100ml/3–4fl oz milk

Grease a 1 litre/2 pint basin, and put 1×15ml spoon/1 tablespoon of golden syrup in the bottom. Sift together the flour, bicarbonate of soda, salt, and ginger. Add the breadcrumbs, suet, and sugar. Beat together the egg, remaining syrup, treacle, and 75ml/3fl oz of the milk. Stir this mixture into the dry ingredients, adding more milk if required, to make a soft dropping consistency. Put into the basin, cover with greased paper or foil and steam for 1½–2 hours. Leave for 5–10 minutes to firm up, then turn out.

Serve with warmed golden syrup and whipped cream.

ROLY-POLY PUDDING

6–7 helpings

300g/10oz plain flour
½×2.5ml spoon/¼ teaspoon salt
2×5ml spoons/2 teaspoons baking
    powder

150g/5oz shredded suet
cold water
flour for dusting
jam for spreading

Sift the flour, salt, and baking powder together. Add the suet, and enough cold water to make a soft but not sticky dough. Roll out into a rectangle about 6mm/¼ inch thick, and spread with jam almost to the edge. Dampen the edges and roll up lightly. Seal the edges. Lay the dough on a scalded, well-floured pudding cloth and tie up the ends of the cloth. Put into a saucepan of fast-boiling water, reduce the heat and simmer for 2–2½ hours. Drain well and unwrap.

Serve sliced, with any sweet sauce.

RAISIN-GRAPE.

CHRISTMAS PUDDING

6 helpings per pudding

fat for greasing
200g/7oz plain flour
a pinch of salt
1×5ml spoon/1 teaspoon ground
  ginger
1×5ml spoon/1 teaspoon mixed
  spice
1×5ml spoon/1 teaspoon grated
  nutmeg
50g/2oz chopped blanched
  almonds
400g/13oz light *or* dark brown sugar

250g/8oz shredded suet
250g/8oz sultanas
250g/8oz currants
200g/7oz seedless raisins
200g/7oz cut mixed peel
175g/6oz stale white breadcrumbs
6 eggs
75ml/3fl oz stout
juice of 1 orange
50ml/2fl oz brandy *or* to taste
125–250ml/¼–½ pint milk

Grease four 625ml/1¼ pint basins, Sift together the flour, salt, ginger, mixed spice, and nutmeg into a mixing bowl. Add the nuts, sugar, suet, sultanas, currants, raisins, peel, and breadcrumbs. Beat together the eggs, stout, orange juice, brandy, and 125ml/¼ pint milk. Stir this into the dry ingredients, adding more milk if required, to give a soft dropping consistency. Put the mixture into the prepared basins, cover with greased paper or foil, and a floured cloth. Put into deep boiling water and boil steadily for 6–7 hours, or half steam for the same length of time.

To store, cover with a clean dry cloth, wrap in greaseproof paper and store in a cool place until required. To re-heat, boil or steam for 1½–2 hours. Serve with Pouring Custard (page 17).

Golden Syrup Pudding

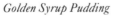

CLOUTIE DUMPLING

—— *4–6 helpings* ——

50g/2oz muscatel raisins
125g/5oz shredded suet
300g/10oz self-raising flour
125g/5oz soft light brown sugar
125g/5oz sultanas
1×5ml spoon/1 teaspoon baking
 powder
1×5ml spoon/1 teaspoon mixed
 spice
1×5ml spoon/1 teaspoon ground
 ginger

1×5ml spoon/1 teaspoon ground
 cinnamon
50g/2oz cut mixed peel
1×2.5ml spoon/½ teaspoon salt
1 medium sized carrot (100g/4oz
 approx) *or* eating apple
125g/5oz black treacle
200ml/8fl oz milk
1 egg.
flour for dusting *or* fat for greasing

De-seed the raisins. Mix the suet, dry ingredients and dried fruit together in a large bowl. Peel the apple if used. Grate the carrot or apple, and add to the dry ingredients. Dissolve the treacle in the milk over low heat. Mix into the dry ingredients to make a fairly soft dropping consistency. Mix in the egg, blending thoroughly.

Put the mixture into a scalded floured cloth, tie with string, allowing room for expansion. Place on a plate in a saucepan and fill up with water to three-quarters of the way up the dumpling. Simmer for 3 hours. Alternatively, steam the dumpling in a 1.5 litre/3 pint greased basin covered with greased paper or foil.

Serve hot or cold with a custard (page 17).

MRS BEETON'S BACHELOR'S PUDDING

—— *5–6 helpings* ——

150g/5oz cooking apples
100g/4oz stale white breadcrumbs
grated rind of ½ lemon
100g/4oz currants
75g/3oz caster sugar
a pinch of salt

½×2.5ml spoon/¼ teaspoon
 grated nutmeg
2 eggs
milk
1×5ml spoon/1 teaspoon baking
 powder
fat for greasing

Peel, core, and chop the apples coarsely. Mix together the breadcrumbs, apples, grated lemon rind, currants, sugar, salt and nutmeg. Beat the eggs until liquid and add to the dry ingredients with enough milk to form a soft dropping consistency. Leave to stand for 30 minutes. Stir in the baking powder. Put the mixture into a greased 1 litre/2 pint basin, cover with greased paper or foil and steam for 2½–3 hours. Leave in the basin for a few minutes, then turn out.

COCOA-BEAN.

CHOCOLATE PUDDING

— 5–6 helpings —

fat for greasing
50g/2oz plain chocolate
125ml/¼ pint milk
40g/1½oz butter *or* margarine
40g/1½oz sugar

2 eggs
100g/4oz stale white breadcrumbs
½×2.5ml spoon/¼ teaspoon
   baking powder

Grease a 750ml/1½ pint basin or 6 dariole moulds. Grate the chocolate into a saucepan, add the milk and heat slowly to dissolve the chocolate. Cream together the fat and sugar. Separate the eggs and beat the yolks into the creamed mixture. Add the melted chocolate, breadcrumbs, and baking powder. Whisk the egg whites until fairly stiff and fold into the mixture. Put into the basin or moulds, cover with greased paper or foil, and steam for 1 hour for a large pudding, and 30 minutes for dariole moulds. Leave in the basin for a few minutes, then turn out.

Cloutie Dumpling

PATRIOTIC PUDDING

6 helpings

fat for greasing
3 × 15ml spoons/3 tablespoons red
   jam
200g/7oz plain flour
a pinch of salt
2 × 5ml spoons/2 teaspoons baking
   powder

100g/4oz butter *or* margarine
100g/4oz caster sugar
1 egg
75ml/3fl oz milk (approx)

Grease a 1 litre/2 pint basin and cover the bottom with the jam. Sift together the flour, salt, and baking powder. Rub the fat into the flour, salt and baking powder. Rub the fat into the flour and add the sugar. Beat the egg and milk together, and stir into the dry ingredients to form a soft dropping consistency. Put the mixture into the basin, cover with greased paper or foil, and steam for 1½–2 hours. Leave in the basin for a few minutes, then turn out.

Serve with the same warmed jam as used in the recipe.

ALMOND PUDDINGS

4–8 helpings

fat for greasing
75g/3oz butter *or* margarine
75g/3oz caster sugar
3 eggs

150g/5oz ground almonds
3 × 15ml spoons/3 tablespoons
   single cream

Grease 8 dariole moulds. Cream together the fat and sugar. Separate the eggs and beat the yolks into the creamed mixture. Stir in the ground almonds and cream. Whisk the egg whites until as stiff as the main mixture, and fold them in lightly. Three-quarters fill the moulds, cover with greased paper or foil, and steam for 45–60 minutes until firm to the touch. Leave in the moulds for a few minutes, then turn out.

Serve with warmed apricot or strawberry jam.

GUARDS PUDDING

4–6 helpings

100g/4oz butter *or* margarine
100g/4oz soft light *or* dark brown
   sugar
3 × 15ml spoons/3 tablespoons
   raspberry *or* strawberry jam
2 eggs
a pinch of salt

100g/4oz brown breadcrumbs
1 × 2.5ml spoon/½ teaspoon
   bicarbonate of soda
1 × 10ml spoon/1 dessertspoon
   warm water
butter for greasing

Cream together the fat and sugar, and beat in the jam. Mix in the eggs, salt, and breadcrumbs. Dissolve the bicarbonate of soda in the warm water and stir into the mixture. Put into a buttered 1 litre/2 pint basin, cover with greased paper or foil, and steam for 3 hours. Leave in the basin for a few minutes, then turn out.

Serve with the same warmed jam as used in the recipe.

COCONUT PUDDING

4–6 helpings

150g/5oz plain flour
a pinch of salt
2 × 15ml spoons/2 teaspoons baking
   powder
50g/2oz butter *or* margarine

50g/2oz caster sugar
50g/2oz desiccated coconut
1 egg
50ml/2fl oz milk (approx)
fat for greasing

Sift together the flour, salt, and baking powder. Rub in the fat, then add the sugar and coconut. Beat the egg and milk together, stir into the dry ingredients, and mix to a soft dropping consistency. Put the mixture into a greased 750ml/1½ pint basin, cover with greased paper or foil and steam for 1½–2 hours. Leave in the basin for a few minutes, then turn out.

PRINCE ALBERT'S PUDDING

6 helpings

400g/13oz prunes
500ml/1 pint water
grated rind of 1 lemon
25g/1oz light soft brown sugar
butter for greasing

100g/4oz butter *or* margarine
100g/4oz caster sugar
2 eggs
40g/1½oz rice flour
100g/4oz brown breadcrumbs

SAUCE

1 × 5ml spoon/1 teaspoon arrowroot
250ml/½ pint prune liquid (see
   Method)

1 × 10ml spoon/1 dessertspoon
   granulated sugar
2–3 drops cochineal

Wash the prunes and soak them in the water overnight. Stew the prunes with half the lemon rind, the water and the brown sugar until soft. Strain and reserve 250ml/½ pint of the liquid for the sauce. Stone and halve the prunes. Line a buttered 1 litre/2 pint basin with the prunes, skin sides against the basin. Chop any prunes which are left over.

Cream together well the fat and caster sugar. Separate the eggs and beat the yolks into the creamed mixture. Add the remaining lemon rind, any chopped prunes, the rice flour, and the breadcrumbs. Whisk the egg whites until fairly stiff and fold into the mixture. Put into the basin, cover with greased paper or foil, and steam for 1½–1¾ hours.

Meanwhile, make the sauce. Blend the arrowroot to a smooth paste with some of the reserved prune liquid. Boil the rest of the liquid, and pour it gradually over the blended arrowroot, stirring all the time. Return to the saucepan, and bring to the boil, stirring all the time. Reduce the heat and simmer for 2–3 minutes. Add the sugar and cochineal.

When the pudding is cooked, leave for a few minutes, then turn out on to a serving dish and pour the sauce over it.

Prince Albert's Pudding

BAKED PUDDINGS

JAM SPONGE PUDDING

— 4–6 helpings —

100g/4oz butter *or* margarine
100g/4oz caster sugar
2 eggs
150g/5oz plain flour
1×5ml spoon/1 teaspoon baking powder

½×2.5ml spoon/¼ teaspoon vanilla essence
2×15ml spoons/2 tablespoons milk (approx)
2×15ml spoons/2 tablespoons jam
fat for greasing

Cream the fat and sugar together until light and fluffy. Beat the eggs until liquid, then beat them gradually into the creamed mixture. Sift together the flour and the baking powder, and fold them in. Add the essence and enough milk to form a soft dropping consistency. Put the jam in the bottom of a greased 1 litre/2 pint pie dish, then add the sponge mixture. Bake in a moderate oven at 180°C/350°F/Gas 4, for 30–35 minutes until well risen and golden-brown.

Serve from the dish with the same warmed jam as used in the recipe.

Note The pie dish can be encircled with a pie frill before presenting at table.

DEVONSHIRE RUM

— 3–4 helpings —

250g/8oz (approx) cold Christmas pudding *or* rich fruit cake
fat for greasing
1 egg
2×10ml spoons/2 dessertspoons cornflour

250ml/½ pint milk
1×10ml spoon/1 dessertspoon soft brown sugar
50ml/2fl oz rum *or* a few drops rum essence

Cut the pudding or cake into fingers, and arrange in a greased 750ml/1½ pint pie dish. Beat the egg until liquid. Mix the cornflour to a paste with a little of the milk. Heat the remaining milk to scalding point, then pour it slowly on to the cornflour, stirring to prevent lumps forming. Return it to the heat and cook gently for 2 minutes; then stir in the sugar, egg, and rum or rum essence. Pour the mixture over the pudding or cake and bake in a moderate oven at 180°C/350°F/Gas 4, for about 30 minutes or until firm.

EVE'S PUDDING

4 helpings

400g/13oz cooking apples
grated rind and juice of 1 lemon
75g/3oz Demerara sugar
1×15ml spoon/1 tablespoon water
fat for greasing

75g/3oz butter *or* margarine
75g/3oz caster sugar
1 egg
100g/4oz self-raising flour

Peel, core, and slice the apples thinly. Mix together with the lemon rind and juice, Demerara sugar and water, and put into a greased 1 litre/2 pint pie dish. Cream the fat and caster sugar together until light and fluffy. Beat the egg until liquid and beat into the creamed mixture over the apples. Bake in a moderate oven at 180°C/350°F/Gas 4, for 40–45 minutes until the apples are soft and the sponge is firm

Serve with Pouring Custard (page 17) or melted apple jelly and single cream.

APPLE CRUMBLE

6 helpings

625g/1¼lb cooking apples
100g/4oz brown sugar
50ml/2fl oz water
grated rind of 1 lemon
fat for greasing

75g/3oz butter *or* margarine
150g/5oz plain flour
75g/3oz caster sugar
½×2.5ml spoon/¼ teaspoon
    ground ginger

Peel, core, and slice the apples. Cook with the brown sugar, water, and lemon rind in a covered pan until soft. Fill a greased 1 litre/2 pint pie dish with the apples. Rub the fat into the flour until it resembles fine breadcrumbs. Add the caster sugar and ginger and stir well, sprinkle the mixture over the apples, and press down lightly. Bake in a moderate oven at 180°C/350°F/Gas 4, for 30–40 minutes until the crumble is golden-brown.

Jam Sponge Pudding

COTTAGE PUDDING

5–6 helpings

200g/7oz plain flour
a pinch of salt
2×5ml spoons/2 teaspoons baking
    powder
100g/4oz butter *or* margarine

75g/3oz soft light brown sugar
100g/4oz raisins
1 egg
50–75ml/2–3fl oz milk
butter for greasing

Sift together the flour, salt, and baking powder. Rub the fat into the flour and add the rest of the dry ingredients. Beat the egg until liquid and stir into the dry ingredients with enough milk to make a soft dropping consistency. Put the mixture into a greased 25×20cm/10×8 inch baking dish and bake in a fairly hot oven at 190°C/375°F/Gas 5, for 35–40 minutes until firm in the centre and golden-brown.

Serve with Pouring Custard (page 17) or any sweet sauce

CASTLE PUDDINGS

3–4 helpings

100g/4oz butter *or* margarine
100g/4oz sugar
2 eggs
½×2.5ml spoon/¼ teaspoon
    vanilla essence

100g/4oz plain flour
1×5ml spoon/1 teaspoon baking
    powder
fat for greasing

Work together the fat and sugar until light and creamy. Beat in the eggs and vanilla essence. Sift together the flour and baking powder, and fold in the creamed mixture. Three-quarters fill 6–8 greased dariole moulds. Bake in a moderate oven at 180°C/350°F/Gas 4, for 20–25 minutes, until set and well risen.

Serve with Pouring Custard (page 17).

EXETER PUDDING

5–6 helpings

butter for greasing
125g/5oz stale white breadcrumbs
25g/1oz ratafias *or* small macaroons
75g/3oz shredded suet
50g/2oz sago
75g/3oz caster sugar
grated rind and juice of 1 lemon

3 eggs
2×15ml spoons/2 tablespoons milk
25ml/1fl oz rum *or* to taste
    (optional)
2 individual sponge cakes
75g/3oz jam (any type)

Butter a 1 litre/2 pint pie dish. Coat with some of the crumbs, and cover the bottom with half the ratafias or macaroons. Mix together the remaining crumbs, suet, sago, sugar, lemon rind, and juice. Beat together the eggs, milk, and rum, if used, and stir into the dry ingredients. Slice the sponge cakes. Put some of the mixture into the dish, cover with slices of sponge cake, a layer of jam, and some of the remaining ratafias. Repeat the layers until all the ingredients are used, finishing with a layer of breadcrumb mixture. Bake in a moderate oven at 180°C/350°F/Gas 4, for 45–60 minutes.

Serve with the same warmed jam as used in the recipe.

Opposite, from the left:
Plums with Port (page 185),
Eve's Pudding (page 181) and
Mrs Beeton's Bachelor's Pudding (page 177)

ALMOND CASTLES

———— *4–8 helpings* ————

75g/3oz butter
75g/3oz caster sugar
3 eggs
3×15ml spoons/3 tablespoons
  single cream *or* milk

1×15ml spoon/1 tablespoon
  brandy (optional)
150g/5oz ground almonds
fat for greasing

Cream together the butter and sugar until light and fluffy. Separate the eggs. Stir the egg yolk, cream or milk, brandy if used, and ground almonds into the creamed mixture. Whisk the egg whites until just stiff, and fold lightly into the mixture. Three-quarters fill 8 greased dariole moulds. Bake in a warm oven at 160°C/325°F/Gas 3, for 20–25 minutes, until the puddings are firm in the centre and golden-brown.

Turn out and serve with Pouring Custard (page 17).

FRUIT PUDDINGS

GOOSEBERRY FRITTERS

———— *4 helpings* ————

400g/13oz gooseberries
oil *or* fat for deep frying

caster sugar

BATTER

50g/2oz plain flour
a pinch of salt
1×15ml spoon/1 tablespoon caster
  sugar

2 eggs
3×15ml spoons/3 tablespoons milk

Prepare the batter first. Sift together the flour and salt. Add the sugar. Separate the eggs. Mix the yolks and milk into the flour and beat well to form a thick batter. Prepare and dry the gooseberries. Heat the fat to 180–185°C/356–365°F. Whisk the egg whites until stiff and fold into the batter. Add the gooseberries. Dip a metal spoon in the hot fat, and then lift 3 coated gooseberries on to it. Lower them into the hot fat, without separating them. As the batter cooks, the berries will fuse together. Fry until golden-brown, turning once. Drain well.

Serve sprinkled with plenty of sugar.

GOOSEBERRY.

PLUMS WITH PORT

6 helpings

1kg/2lb plums
100–150g/4–5oz soft light brown
 sugar

150ml/6fl oz port

Cut the plums neatly in half and remove the stones. Put into a baking dish or casserole, sprinkle with the sugar (the amount required will depend on the sweetness of the plums) and pour port on top. Cover securely with a lid or foil and bake in a cool oven at 150°C/300°F/Gas 2, for 45–60 minutes or until the plums are tender. Serve hot, or lightly chilled.

TOFFEE-TOPPED GRAPE CREAM

4 helpings

250g/8oz grapes
fat for greasing
250ml/½ pint double cream

2×15ml spoons/2 tablespoons
 brandy (optional)
3–4×15ml spoons/3–4 tablespoons
 Demerara sugar

Halve and de-pip the grapes, and put into a greased ovenproof dish. Whip the cream until it holds its shape, then spread it over the grapes. Chill in a refrigerator for at least 8 hours. Just before serving, sprinkle with the brandy and sugar, put under a moderately hot grill for 3–4 minutes until the sugar melts and bubbles.

Almond Castles

STUFFED FRESH PEACHES

4–8 helpings

50g/2oz unsalted butter
8 large peaches
50g/2oz salted butter
125g/5oz caster sugar
125g/5oz ground almonds
125g/5oz plain *or* sponge cake
  crumbs

2 egg whites
2 drops almond essence *or* 1×15ml
  spoon/1 tablespoon anisette
  liqueur

Grease a shallow ovenproof dish with the unsalted butter. With the point of a knife, make 2 slits in the skin of each peach. Scald the fruit for 40 seconds, drain and peel. Cut in half and remove the stones carefully without spoiling the shape. Place the peaches on the dish, hollows uppermost. Melt the salted butter. Mix the sugar, ground almonds, and crumbs with most of the melted butter. Add the egg whites and the essence or liqueur and beat the mixture to a creamy consistency. Using a piping bag or spoon, fill the hollow of each peach with the mixture. Brush with the remaining butter and bake in a moderate oven at 180°C/350°F/Gas 4, for 20 minutes.

Serve hot with ice cream.

PEARS IN WINE

4 helpings

100g/4oz white sugar
250ml/½ pint water
2×15ml spoons/2 tablespoons
  redcurrant jelly
1×2.5cm/1 inch piece cinnamon
  stick

4 large ripe cooking pears (500g/1lb
  approx)
250ml/½ pint red wine
25g/1oz blanched almonds
a few drops red food colouring
  (optional)

Put the sugar, water, redcurrant jelly, and cinnamon stick into a pan and heat gently until the sugar and jelly have dissolved. Peel the pears, leaving the stalks in place. Carefully remove as much of the core as possible without breaking the fruit. Add the pears to the pan, cover, and simmer gently for 15 minutes. Remove the pears carefully, arrange them on a serving dish and keep warm.

Remove the cinnamon stick. Shred the almonds and add to the pan. Boil the liquid remaining in the pan rapidly until it is reduced to a thin syrup. Add a few drops of red food colouring if the colour is not deep enough. Pour the syrup over the pears and serve warm, with fresh single or double cream.

This dessert can also be served cold. Pour the hot syrup over the pears, leave to cool, then chill before serving.

Note The pears can be baked in a very cool oven at 120°C/250°F/Gas ½, for 4–5 hours.

CHERRIES JUBILÉE

4 helpings

50g/2oz sugar
250ml/½ pint water
500g/1 lb dark red fresh cherries

2×5ml spoons/2 teaspoons
  arrowroot
4×15ml spoons/4 tablespoons
  Kirsch

In the kitchen, make a sugar syrup with the sugar and water. Stone the cherries. Poach them in the syrup until just tender, then drain and cool. Reserve the syrup. Blend the arrowroot with a very little of the syrup, then stir it into the remainder. Pour into a saucepan and bring to the boil, stirring all the time. Boil for 3–5 minutes until thickened and syrupy. Arrange the cherries in individual heatproof serving bowls and pour the thickened syrup over them. Take the bowls and the Kirsch to the table.

At the table, warm the Kirsch in a small jug or ladle. Pour 1×15ml spoon/1 tablespoon of it over each helping, light it, and serve while still alight if possible.

Note This famous dish was originally created for Queen Victoria's Diamond Jubilee.

Stuffed Fresh Peaches

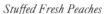

BANANAS IN RUM

— 4 helpings —

4 large bananas
3×15ml spoons/3 tablespoons soft
    brown sugar
1×2.5ml spoon/½ teaspoon
    ground cinnamon

25g/1oz butter
3–4×15ml spoons/3–4 tablespoons
    rum

In the kitchen, cut the bananas in half lengthways, and put them flat on a plate. If this is done some time before the dish is cooked, sprinkle the bananas with a little lemon juice to prevent the fruit turning brown. Mix together the soft brown sugar and the cinnamon. Take all the ingredients to the table.

At the table, sprinkle the bananas with the sugar and cinnamon mixture. Melt the butter in a blazer or frying pan, and fry the bananas flat side down for 1–2 minutes until lightly browned underneath. Turn them over carefully, sprinkle with any remaining sugar and cinnamon, and continue frying. When the bananas are soft but not mushy, pour the rum over them. Tilt and baste, then light the rum; baste again. Scrape any caramelized sugar from the base of the pan and stir it into the rum. Shake the pan gently until the flames die down.

Arrange the bananas on warmed serving plates, pour the rum sauce over them and serve with double cream.

APPLE CHARLOTTE

— 5–6 helpings —

butter for greasing
400g/13oz cooking apples
grated rind and juice of 1 lemon
100g/4oz soft light brown sugar
a pinch of ground cinnamon

50–75g/2–3oz butter
8–10 large slices white bread,
    6mm/¼ inch thick
1×15ml spoon/1 tablespoon caster
    sugar

Grease a 1 litre/2 pint charlotte mould or 16.25cm/6½ inch cake tin heavily with butter. Peel, core, and slice the apples. Simmer the apples, lemon rind and juice with the sugar and cinnamon until the apples soften to a thick purée. Leave to cool.

Melt the butter. Cut the crusts off the bread, and dip 1 slice in the butter. Cut it into a round to fit the bottom of the mould or tin. Fill any spaces if necessary. Dip the remaining bread slices in the butter. Line the inside of the mould with 6 slices, touching one another. Fill the bread case with the cooled purée. Complete the case by fitting the top with more bread slices. Cover loosely with greased paper or foil, and bake in a moderate oven at 180°C/350°F/Gas 4, for 40–45 minutes. For serving, turn out and dredge with caster sugar.

Serve with bramble jelly and cream.

APPLE AND BLOSSOM.

BAKED APPLES STUFFED WITH RICE AND NUTS

6 helpings

6 medium-sized cooking apples
25g/1oz flaked almonds *or* other
  nuts
40g/1½oz seedless raisins
25–50g/1–2oz boiled rice
  (preferably boiled in milk)

1 egg
50g/2oz sugar *or* to taste
2×15ml spoons/2 tablespoons
  butter
raspberry *or* blackcurrant syrup

Wash and core the apples but do not peel them. With a small rounded spoon, hollow out part of the flesh surrounding the core hole. Do not break the outside skin. Mix together the nuts, raisins, and rice, using enough rice to make a stuffing for all the apples. Beat the egg until liquid. Add the sugar to the rice and nuts, and enough egg to bind the mixture; melt and add the butter. Fill the apples with the rice mixture. Place in a baking tray, and add 6mm/¼ inch depth hot water. Bake in a fairly hot oven at 190°C/375°F/Gas 5, for 40 minutes or until the apples are tender. Remove from the oven and place on a warmed serving platter. Warm the fruit syrup and pour it over the apples.

    Serve with chilled cream or sweetened yoghurt.

Bananas in Rum

APPLE AMBER

4 helpings

3 eggs
1×15ml spoon/1 tablespoon lemon
 juice

500ml/1 pint thick apple purée
250g/8oz caster sugar (approx)

DECORATION

glacé cherries

angelica

Separate the eggs. Beat the lemon juice and yolks into the apple purée with about 75g/3oz of the sugar. Turn into a 750ml/1½ pint baking dish, cover, and bake in a moderate oven at 180°C/350°F/Gas 4, for 15 minutes. Whisk the egg whites until they form stiff peaks. Gradually whisk in 150g/5oz of the remaining sugar, adding 1×5ml spoon/1 teaspoon at a time. Pile the meringue on top of the apple mixture and sprinkle with 1×15ml spoon/1 tablespoon sugar. Return to the oven and bake for a further 15 minutes or until the meringue is pale golden-brown.

Serve at once with Pouring Custard (page 17) or single cream.

ALMOND & BLOSSOM.